Continental Taste

Camden History Society
Occasional paper 2

This publication has been made possible by a grant from
The Scouloudi Foundation in association
with the Institute of Historical Research
and through support from the Unione Ticinese

Designed by Ivor Kamlish

Editor of publications F Peter Woodford
ISBN 0-904491-37-4

Cover Dining room at Monico's, Piccadilly c. 1910
[Courtesy of Westminster Libraries]

The photograph conveys the luxurious surroundings, with
large mirrors, carved woodwork. starched table linen,
silvered cutlery and vases surmounting the cruets.

Opposite A Ticinese café proprietor and his staff c. 1875

The photograph illustrates the close links between chocolate
making, a tradition in the upper Blenio valley, and the
café-restaurant trade. The men standing first and second
to the left hold traditional, and by then already obsolescent,
chocolate and coffee-making implements. What appears
to be the circular base to the bucket was the stone 'Prea',
a concave serrated surface on which coffee or chocolate
beans were placed to be crushed. The man standing second
to the left carries the stone rolling pin. The bucket contained
milk to dilute the liquid from the beans. The youth kneeling
at the front can have been barely 14 years old. One of the
group must be a member of the Biucchi family, who ran
their own cafe-restaurants in London at different times.
[Peter Jacomelli archive]

Continental Taste

Ticinese emigrants
and their Café-Restaurants in Britain
1847-1987

by Peter Barber *and* Peter Jacomelli

Contents

Introduction

In 1901 a London guidebook commented on 'the innumerable and generally well-ordered Italian-Swiss restaurants which meet the eye in almost every leading London thoroughfare'.[1] In fact, they were to be found throughout Great Britain. Though they were particularly numerous in and around London (in Oxford Street alone at that time there were seven),[2] they also existed in most of the resort towns along the South Coast. They ranged in type from the large and opulent to the small and tawdry, but they had a generic similarity which in more ways than one could be called a family likeness.

The last of the restaurants passed out of Ticinese hands in 1987. They have fallen into general oblivion, but they played a distinct if minor role in British social history. They provided the first cafés and restaurants to cater for the sensibilities and appetites of its middle and lower-middle classes at a time when these groups were emerging as a major force in British society. In one respect their modern successors are the ubiquitous Italian, Chinese and Indian restaurants. In another it is *McDonalds* and its predecessors such as the *Lyons Corner Houses* - which, in more than one case, took over the premises vacated by the Ticinesi after 1930.

1. The Leventina valley (left) and Blenio valley (right) in 1858 (at a scale of 1:100,000). A masterpiece of relief mapping, the 'Dufour' map of Switzerland gives a superb impression of the mountainous, wooded terrain, of the barren river beds and the scattering of small villages. [By courtesy of the British Library]

The Background: Ticino, Lombardy and France 1600-1847

The roots of the 'Swiss café and restaurant' can be found in the culture and history of the northernmost valleys of the Swiss canton of Ticino: the Valle Leventina and, particularly, the Val di Blenio (fig. 1). These lead southwards from the Gotthard and Lukmanier passes respectively. Like many other mountainous areas, the valleys had a tradition of seasonal male emigration. The combination of a relatively large population and a barren soil that was subject to landslide, storm and flood left little alternative if a family was to survive. It has been calculated that as late as 1847 52% of the male population eligible for military service was absent during the autumn and winter months. Elsewhere in Ticino the percentage was never higher than 35%.[3] The prolonged absence of most of the men of working age affected almost every aspect of village life. Childbirth was restricted to certain seasons. Since seasonal emigrants were still expected to play a full part in the affairs of their communities, the timing of local assemblies was arranged to meet their convenience. The burden of agricultural work and the maintenance of family life fell far more heavily on women than it did in rural communities better endowed by nature elsewhere in Western Europe.

Chestnuts grow in profusion in the valleys of Canton Ticino. For centuries the men from the lower, southern part of the Val di Blenio and from the Leventina had gained an income from selling roast chestnuts on the streets of northern Italian towns. Their fellows from farther up the Val di Blenio, by contrast, had specialised as chocolate-makers and chocolate sellers since at least the mid-18th century.[4] All must have had some experience of offering board and lodging to travellers coming to or going from the Gotthard or the Lukmanier - another tradition that could be utilised abroad.

From humble beginnings as sellers of chestnuts, chocolates and pastries at street corners many emigrants to Northern Italy went on to prosper. They became owners of kiosks selling fruit and wine in addition to chestnuts, tavern owners (recorded as early as 1602), wholesale importers of fruit and vegetables, and chocolate manufacturers. For every chestnut or chocolate vendor there were several still more humble people engaged as porters or helpers. Tavern owners needed waiters, and chocolate manufacturers required workers in their factories. Established chestnut or chocolate vendors naturally looked to their relatives and compatriots to fill these positions.[5]

The chestnut sellers tended to return from the Italian cities to their home villages for the harvest every summer. Although of necessity the tavern owners, chestnut wholesalers and chocolate manufacturers could not do this each year, they maintained their links with their native villages and regularly sent money home. In the fullness of time and flushed with success they retired there. Like their fellows in Rome, Florence, Genoa, Livorno or Turin, the Leventina porters in Milan formed a society or 'compagnia'. It represented their interests vis-à-vis outsiders, provided some social life and lent mutual support in sickness, in health and, for all too many, in death. In a more positive spirit the compagnie also financed improvements in their home villages, such as repairs to the church and the creation of altar cloths.[6]

From the very beginning the 'padrone' was the essential link between the village and its emigrants. In most cases, he would work from abroad, summoning relatives and friends to his place of work.[7] The more successful padroni, however, continued to provide employment after their return to their native villages. One such man was Giovanni Martino Soldini (1747-1831). From his home in Olivone, in the middle of the Val di Blenio, he ran a commercial network based on chocolate and spices that embraced most of Europe between Amsterdam, Prague and Milan. As well as providing work for Bleniesi he also provided credit for them and even undertook to trace missing compatriots in the East Indies![8]

By 1850, the Bleniesi and Leventinesi still predominantly emigrated to Lombardy and particularly to Milan, with a few going to other Italian regions. A number had, however, long emigrated to German, Spanish, Netherlandish and French towns and in the course of the early 19th century the number going to France continually grew.[9] The Ticinesi came to form the largest group of Swiss registered in Paris, and the Bleniesi and Leventinesi dominated the Ticinese group.[10] Certain villages, particularly Dangio, Dongio, Olivone, Malvaglia, Semione and Aquila, had become associated with emigration to France and Belgium by as early as 1800. From the later 18th century onwards, the Bleniesi opened their own enterprises in the larger European cities. One such, the *Café Corazza* in Paris owned by the Corazza family of Dongio, became notorious as a meeting place for Jacobins during the French Revolution.[11] Stefano Gatti (1776-1842) who came of a patrician family, also from Dongio, began a wholesale chestnut and later fruit and vegetable importing company, *Righenzi et Gatti*.[12] Other chestnut importers included the *Grand Dépot Mazzucchi* and *Monico e Fratelli* (again from Dongio) in Paris, or the Guidotti company, originally of Semione, which operated in Lyon (a big centre for men from Dangio), Mulhouse and Strasbourg.[13]

In most respects, then, the patterns to be followed by the Bleniesi and Leventinesi in Britain were long established by 1847. At that time, however, only a few had crossed the Channel.[14] It was political, social, industrial and cultural developments inside mid-19th century Western Europe that changed this. First and foremost, the possibilities for employment in Italy had been drying up since 1815 following the abolition of the traditional monopolies enjoyed by Ticinesi in Italy, such as those of Locarnesi porters in the ports of Genoa, Pisa and Livorno.[15] The expulsion of the Ticinesi from Lombardy by the Austrians in 1853, in reprisal for Ticinese support for *carbonari* and other Italian nationalists, particularly hit the emigrants from the Val di Blenio.[16]

The obvious alternative, France, became a much less attractive destination in the same years. It was in economic recession and political turmoil in the 1840s and there are indications that the market for Ticinese *marronai* and café owners in France was also beginning to become sated.[17] Ticinese emigration from France was further encouraged by the xenophobic hostility exhibited towards all foreigners, but particularly the poor immigrant workers, when the economy failed to improve immediately after the 1848 revolution.[18]

London, the largest, richest and most dynamic city in 19th-century Europe, however, offered distinct possibilities. The opening of railways with relatively low fares made it easily accessible from Paris even for the poor in the later 1840s. The noticeable weakness of many Englishmen for all manifestations of French culture made it still more attractive. In the following decades many Ticinesi arrived in London from France, but continued to maintain close links with friends and relatives on the other side of the Channel.[19]

English taste *and the Gattis*

On arrival in England, the Bleniesi and Leventinesi made for the poor and crowded Italian quarter of London. This was centred on Saffron Hill between Holborn, Clerkenwell and the Gray's Inn Road, west of the City of London and east of Westminster.[20] Conditions were notoriously insanitary and dirty, but boarding houses were plentiful and cheap. Moreover it was here that other Ticinesi lived. They pursued trades typical of those of the Italian community as a whole, such as the manufacturing and selling of artificial flowers, figurines and mirrors, or as barometer makers (a profession particularly associated with the shores of Lake Como) like the Fattorini family from Chiasso.[21] There were, as yet, however, few Italians who were active in catering, despite a dramatic increase in the overall number of 'confectioners and pastrycooks' recorded in Kelly's Post Office Directories for London in the course of the 1840s.

This was to change with the arrival in England in July 1847[22] of Carlo Gatti (1817-1878) of Marogno, near Dongio in the Val di Blenio. Carlo, the youngest son of Stefano Gatti, had walked from Dongio to Paris, reputedly with only 25 francs in his pocket, in 1829. Despite his family's strong connections with the French capital, he had not made a success of life there.[23] Even before his arrival in England, however, he seems to have had an inkling that catering represented a great window of opportunity for the Bleniesi and Leventinesi, with their chocolate-making and chestnut-selling traditions and with their recent experience of the best of the Parisian cafés and the exquisite pastries associated with them.

Some Continental culinary concepts were known of in England well before Carlo Gatti's arrival. The word 'ice[d] cream' had been found since 1688; 'café' is first

2. Carlo Gatti's restaurant and (behind) music hall, Villiers Street, in about 1885-1890. Rudyard Kipling, who lived opposite, above Harris the Sausage King, at exactly this time could see into Gatti's Music Hall from his desk. He later recalled 'the smoke, the roar and the good-fellowship of relaxed humanity at Gatti's' to which admittance cost fourpence 'which included a pewter of beer or porter'. He also remembered the music hall artistes 'arguing beneath my window with their cab-drivers as they sped from Hall to Hall'(Rudyard Kipling, *Something of Myself* (London: Macmillan, 1937), pp.79-81. [By courtesy of the Guildhall Library, Corporation of London]

recorded in England in 1816 and 'restaurant' in 1827.[24] The concept of eating good-quality food in comfortable surroundings had also been realised in the gentlemens' clubs of London which had been coming into existence since the middle of the 18th century. There was an excellent French restaurant, *Verrey's* (founded by a Swiss of that name), flourishing in Regent's Street in the 1840s. Some hotels supplied reasonable food. Hotels, restaurants and clubs were, however, the preserves of the extremely wealthy and well-established, and ice cream was a prized delicacy.[25]

In the lower price brackets, London could offer about 200 inns, 400 taverns and 500 coffee houses.[26] There were some cheap, unpleasant foreign establishments in the neighbourhood of Leicester Square, and elsewhere chop houses and dining rooms, cookshops and eating houses 'where nameless nastinesses were always forthcoming, at a cost within the reach of even the poorest, but where the general surroundings were not seldom of a nature to destroy the appetites even of the least fastidious and most penurious'.[27] There were no moderately priced restaurants or cafés in the modern sense of the word. None of the existing establishments were suitable for women or families. Nor did even the cleaner ones meet the expectations of an increasingly demanding and cultured professional class. In most of them the extremely plain cooking, when it was available, consisted of simple steaks, pies and cuts of meat[28] and matched the drabness of the surroundings.

Carlo Gatti set to work from the moment of his arrival. He seems to have begun by selling light pastries (*goffres*) from a stall in Battersea Fields. Within a matter of

months he had earned enough from this delicacy to rent a shop in Hatton Wall, a narrow street north of Hatton Garden in the middle of the Italian quarter.[29] In the autumn and winter of 1847-8, Carlo rented his first pastry shop/café in the Great Hall of Hungerford Market.[30] By 1849 he had acquired two further shops at 29 and 61 Great Hall. Felicity Kinross has shown that in the same months he acquired a café, with Battista Bolla (b.1819) (another native of the Val di Blenio) at 129 Holborn Hill, and a chocolate factory at 122 Holborn Hill, on either side of Leather Lane and about 5 minutes' walk to the south of Hatton Wall.[31] At about the same time, Carlo seems to have begun the large-scale manufacture of ice cream which was sold in the streets, in glasses, at a penny or halfpenny a time. He was probably the first person in England to bring ice cream within the reach of the masses.[32]

3. Agostino and Stefano Gatti, in about 1875, when they had become wealthy enough to move to Beckenham from their previous accommodation above the Royal Adelaide Gallery.

During the 1850s, the Hungerford Great Hall cafés (at various locations within the complex) were administered in partnership first (1855) with Agostino Gatti, probably a cousin, and from 1859 with his brother Giuseppe and another Bleniese from Dongio, Giuseppe Monico.[33] In addition Carlo acquired cafés at 254 Oxford Street, 90 Whitechapel High Street in the East End of London (both first recorded in 1855) and at 7 Edgware Road (1856).[34] After the demolition of Hungerford Market to make way for Charing Cross Station in August 1862, Carlo and his brothers Giuseppe (1807-1873) and Giovanni (1809-1876)[35] purchased 212-4 Westminster Bridge Road. There they opened a restaurant (1862) and, in 1864, *Gatti's Palace of Varieties* alias *Gatti's-over-the-Water* alias *Gattis-in-the-Road*.[36] In the same year Carlo began a café-patisserie at 52 The Strand, then one of London's most elegant streets. With the completion of the new Charing Cross Station, Carlo could return to at least the site of the Hungerford Market. October 1866 saw the opening of grand billiard rooms and *Gatti's Charing Cross Music Hall* alias *the Hungerford Hall* alias *Gatti's-under-the-Arches* at 10-12 Villiers Street beneath the station.[37] For good measure he bought a further café, the *Café Restaurant de la Confédération Suisse*, at 20 Villiers Street (fig. 2). Carlo's account at Coutts Bank also lists income from a *Queen's Head Tavern* that he must also have owned somewhere in London. In addition to these, by 1857, Carlo independently owned an ice importing business on the Regent's Canal at New Wharf Road. The impulse for this may have stemmed from his ice-cream making, but it soon became Carlo's principal source of income.[38]

As well as his music hall activity, Giuseppe was principally involved with chocolate manufacturing. In 1852 he and his brothers founded 'Gatti Brothers' with its factory at Acton Street in Haggerston (Shoreditch), east London.[39] In the next year, Giuseppe created a chocolate factory of his own, initially with its own café, at 13 Aldgate in the City of London. In 1856 he opened a separate café a few doors away at 18 Aldgate, closing down the one at 13 Aldgate, which became a chocolate factory pure and simple.[40] For a period in the 1850s he had other chocolate factories at 67 Blackman Street and at 9 Silver Street in Greenwich.[41] If Pino Peduzzi is to be believed, Giuseppe Gatti owned another music hall, *Gatti's Grand*, at Clapham Junction in South-West London.[42]. He seems also to have acquired the *Hotel du Continent* at 151-2 (later 158-9) Bute Street, Cardiff.[43]

Giovanni Gatti's sons Agostino (1841-1897) and Stefano (1844-1906), born in Paris and Dongio respectively (fig. 3), came over to England with their father in the early 1850s and began their careers when teenagers as waiters at the Hungerford Market.[44] From the very first they seem to have been inseparable. In May 1862, when the Market's demolition was imminent, they and Giuseppe Monico's son Giacomo (1840-1910) opened their own small café at the *Royal Adelaide Gallery* with a narrow frontage at 7/8 Adelaide Street just off the Strand.[45] At first they did not diversify their interests as their uncles had. After the departure in 1872 of Giacomo Monico, who was said[46] to have been more cautious than his partners, however, the operations of the two brothers expanded dramatically. The autumn promenade concerts which they organised between 1873 and 1880 at the Covent Garden Theatre, and the pantomimes mounted in the same theatre in the winters of 1878-1880, showed them how profitable such popular entertainments could be.[47] Their account with Coutts Bank demonstrates that in the same decade they already had some sort of financial arrangement with the Alhambra and Adelphi theatres, and the acquisition of the Adelphi and Vaudeville Theatres duly followed in 1879 and 1892 respectively.[48] It can be inferred from Peduzzi that Agostino and Stefano were also major stake holders in a syndicate, the Variety Theatres Consolidated, which ran four further theatres/music halls, including the Walthamstow Palace and the Chelsea Palace.[49] Until 1896, Agostino and Stefano actively managed the two theatres they directly owned. The emphasis was on melodrama at the Adelphi and light comedy at the Vaudeville: precisely the type of drama likely to appeal to the middle-class clientèle of their café-restaurants.[50]

It is likely that the profits from the promenade concerts enabled the brothers to upgrade the scope of the Royal Adelaide Gallery from 1878[51] and to expand elsewhere. In 1879 they opened a restaurant[52] at the side of the Adelphi Theatre. In 1882-3 they enormously expanded the Royal Adelaide Gallery in a way that had been pioneered at the *Café Royal* (1865)[53] and by their uncle Carlo at his new Hungerford Hall (1866). It gained an additional, grand entrance on William IV Street and a smaller frontage to the Strand. The interior, on several floors, included a beer hall and a variety of increasingly elegant eating rooms as well as the original café.[54] By this time Agostino and Stefano's restaurants were quite distinct from and were running in competition with the concerns directed by their cousins, the children of Carlo and Giuseppe.

It was in the context of the expanded Royal Adelaide Galley that the brothers first got involved with the electricity supply industry. In order to provide the restaurant with electric light and power, which was becoming increasingly *de rigueur* in large establishments, they installed an electricity substation in its cellars in 1882. Three years later, finding that no company would supply the Adelphi Theatre with electric light because of a bylaw prohibiting the laying of electric cables in the Strand during daylight hours, they had cables laid along the Strand at night, opening another substation in Bull Inn court, Maiden Lane, in 1888. The Adelphi became the first London theatre to be lit with electric light. In 1889, capitalising on their success, the brothers created the Charing Cross and Strand Electricity Supply Corporation Ltd and built a power station at Bow. By 1900 the company was providing the City and most of Westminster with electricity.[55]

The enterprises of the Gatti family were of enormous importance for the growth of the Ticinese community in England because of the employment that they generated. It has been calculated that at its height after 1882, the Royal Adelaide Gallery alone employed between 180 and 200 waiters and 40 chefs.[56] In addition, as the census returns reveal, several other trades such as carpenters, billiard markers, bricklayers, icemen, glaziers, confectioners, and later electricians, were also to be found in the restaurants or other Gatti concerns.

Not that all the Ticinesi were directly or even indirectly employed by the Gattis. From the outset the Ticinesi were involved in a wide variety of occupations. In addition to ice merchants, confectioners and restaurateurs and glaziers, there were also coppersmiths[57] and even street labourers.[58] But it was the restaurateurs, chefs and waiters who were particularly numerous and most characteristic. It was also they who tended to retain their distinctive Ticinese character longest.[59]

The Gattis offered more than employment in their numerous concerns. In 1870 Carlo claimed that from the early 1850s, 'he invited several of his countrymen over to England, and, renting shops in different parts of London, he gave them a fair start in this new article of trade, and thus put them in the way of achieving their own independence'.[60] In later years he also gave some large loans to compatriots, such as the Cizzio, Agostino Berti and the Pazzis, to get started in business[61] and smaller loans to other Ticinese restaurateurs and confectioners who may have been in temporary difficulty.[62]

Giuseppe Gatti also helped by advancing money at low rates of interest.[63] His successors and those of his brothers continued to assist their compatriots in similar ways. The accounts of Agostino and Stefano Gatti at Coutts show that until the early 1890s they regularly gave loans to their compatriots. While Carlo Zeglio, who had a confectioner's at 51 Chalk Farm Road, received £40 and Carlo Genoni, who had an establishment in Wimbledon, received only £38 4s 6d in 1879, Giuseppe Odone, who was soon to open a restaurant in Victoria Street, received a number of payments amounting to over £300 in the course of 1888 and in the same year Francesco Gallizia, whose restaurant in Brighton was in operation by 1891, received £400. By 1876, and often thanks to the Gattis, there were numerous Ticinesi like Marco Ferrari, probably from Semione, who had been able to set up business at 11 Kew Road, Richmond, as an 'English and Foreign Ice Merchant. Wholesale and Retail. Ices of every description made to order. Families waited on regularly'.[64]

Sturdy aliens and poor lads[65]: *Getting started in London*

Between 1850 and 1880 some Ticinesi must have arrived in England directly from Ticino, rather than after a prolonged stay in Paris, in order to benefit from Carlo Gatti's benevolence. Their journey would have been long, wearisome and, unless they were prepared to walk (which a few still did), very expensive: the equivalent of 6 months of a waiter's earnings.[66] It involved travel by coach (diligence) over the Gotthard,[67] boat along the length of Lake Lucerne and then coach, train and ferry to London. Yet even this and the prospect of not seeing one's wife and family for years were better than penury and starvation at home. For in these years the Val di Blenio was badly hit by bad weather, adding a further spur to emigration. The richest land on the floor of the valley was swept away by floods in 1868. Conditions hardly improved in the following years. There was another devastating flood in 1907.

The opening of the Gotthard Tunnel in 1882 brought less economic benefit to Canton Ticino than had been hoped, because of the high tariffs imposed on the passage of goods through it. It did, however, open an all-weather direct rail link between Biasca, at the junction of the Blenio and Leventina valleys, and London, and considerably reduced the cost of travel.[68] The Bleniesi and Leventinesi were quick to take advantage of this escape route from poverty. The Tunnel unleashed a flood of emigration from Ticino that was to continue into the opening years of the 20th century. London was the first place of work for most, though the suburbs of London and the British provinces seem to have been the ultimate destinations of these later arrivals.[69]

The new arrivals were predominantly young men, aged between 17 and 24, though some were as young as 14 and a few as old as 48. Between 1851 and 1881 the average age of waiters in the Gatti establishments was 23 years and 7 months. There is some evidence that the average age decreased in each decade after 1860, presumably as more and younger boys came straight from Ticino without pausing for a year or more to work in France.[70] They probably arrived clutching no more than a few coins and various letters of recommendation or simply slips of paper containing useful addresses[71] (fig. 4). At first the Gattis installed them in cheap lodging houses in the Covent Garden or Soho areas.[72] The newcomers often remained there even after they found employment, if there was no room for them in the dormitories over the central London restaurants where they worked.[73] Conditions were spartan and crowded, with as many as 180 crammed together in the same building and with beds being shared.[74]

They worked hard. Giuseppe Giuliani from Aquila in the Val di Blenio, who had recently begun working at the Royal Adelaide Gallery, wrote to his parents in 1908 'Work begins at 8 am and finishes at half-past midnight except on Saturday when it finishes at midnight and Sundays, at 11 pm. Every other day I'm off between 3.30 pm and 6 pm and every day from 10 am till 11.30'.[75] This made a working day of 14½ hours on several days of the week and never less than 10 on the occasional Sunday. Chefs in the Royal Adelaide Gallery, moreover, spent their time working underground in the basement kitchens. Chefs did get paid. Waiters rarely did, and even then the pay tended to be minimal and irregular.[76] They depended on their tips to survive. Some waiters even paid their employers for the right to work well-placed tables. All the while they were separated from their immediate family,[77] and many of the older waiters and chefs did not see their wives for years on end.[78] To add to their woes there was the cold, grey, foggy, wet and windy English weather, which understandably became a regular source of comment in their letters.[79]

Yet the waiters seem to have accepted these conditions with little complaint. If their lodgings left much to be desired, they were at least free and the food seems to have been good, plentiful - and free. Giuseppe Giuliani was positively glowing in his praise of the food that he received at the Royal Adelaide Gallery. 'As far as food is concerned, I am better off than I was at home. In the morning there's coffee or milk or chocolate. At midday there's meat, pasta, salad and everything you want'[80]. On their few days off the waiters, chefs and owners of the smaller cafés got together at social centres resembling Ticinese *osterie* to play *bocce* (bowls) and *scopa* (cards) and to meet their friends.[81] If they needed to buy anything , be it 'kitchen utensils, boots, slippers, wooden shoes or *sabots*, vests or overalls, cigarette papers, caps [or] dress shirt-fronts', they would find it in general stores in Soho which catered for their specific needs and where Italian was spoken.[82]

After 1874, too, the Unione Ticinese was available to provide Swiss-Italian immigrants both with care when ill and with a social life when well. It seems to have grown out of a mutual benefit society for Gatti employees founded by Stefano Gatti in 1870[83] and extended to include the whole Ticinese colony. Among the founder members there were numerous confectioners and owners of smaller cafés and restaurants, and a few of the more senior waiters at the Gatti establishments. In fact there seems to have been little difference in the social standing of these groups. Some confectioners had very small businesses indeed and employed only a couple of waiters, who were frequently relatives. On the other hand some of the senior waiters, such as Stefano Protti, briefly owned cafés before returning to waitering.[84] In addition to waiters, some chocolate and icemakers from other Gatti enterprises were also members, among them Angelo De Grussa who worked at the Royal Adelaide Gallery,[85] and Venanzio Monighetti who worked at the New Wharf Road ice wells.[86]

From the start and for the first few decades, however, the Unione was dominated by the padroni who owned the largest restaurants, notably the Gattis, Mario and Tebaldo Pagani and Giacomo and Battista Monico. They ran the new society in a paternalistic fashion. They furnished all the officers and committee members, and held regular dinners at each other's restaurants at prices beyond the purses of their staff or the poorer café and restaurant owners.[87] At the same time the padroni also supplied the new society with considerable sums of money - in 1881 Agostino and Stefano gave £345[88] - so that membership could provide considerable benefits for the more lowly members. A sickness benefit was payable.[89] Furthermore, from 1881 in return for an annual payment of two guineas (£2 2s) the Charing Cross Hospital undertook to admit any member who needed hospital treatment, if there was a free bed.[90] In 1878 the society purchased a cemetery plot at the Roman Catholic Cemetery in Kensal Green[91] (fig. 5).

Few if any of the Ticinesi intended to settle in England. As a contemporary English writer observed, they

'emigrate from their romantic valleys to our foggy shores and work out their three, four or five years in an alien land, partly for the sake of better wages, partly for that of learning the English language - an accomplishment without which no foreign waiter is considered fully equipped. With unsparing thrift, they save the greater part of their wages; and they acquire the language as quickly as they can; with these two

4. A slip of paper carried by a member of the Genoni family on his arrival in London in about 1860 containing the address of Giuseppe Gatti's chocolate factory in the 'Cyti'. [Peter Jacomelli archive]

possessions they return to their own country, where they may either at once demand a higher salary - or, if they are already well-to-do, buy a smallholding and "settle down"....they... have before them, through all their struggles and hardships, the thought of the peaceful mountain home and honest competency that shall be theirs in middle age.'[92]

The waiters would have laughed at the sentimental language, but essentially they would not have disagreed. Their own letters testify to the advantages they saw in learning English[93] and the extent to which they saved. They needed to, in order to send money back to their relatives in Switzerland and to pay for their own trips there. Most seem, mentally, never to have left their home valleys. In their letters home they give relatives advice on the finer points of agriculture and viticulture,[94] on financial matters,[95] on household repairs,[96] on the conduct of negotiations over the sale of land, animals, buildings and legacies[97]. They repeatedly send money and goods to their families[98] and in at least one case try to get scythes made more cheaply than in Ticino.[99]

Their relationship with their employers varied. At times, they were almost touchingly loyal, even to the extent of sending wishes for their recovery (when Stefano Gatti fell ill while in Switzerland) or asking their relatives to send over edelweiss for them.[100] At times, however, exhaustion brought on by long hours of work, a fiery temperament and a perpetual shortage of money resulted in explosions on the floor of the restaurant. In about 1870, when working as a waiter at Carlo Gatti's café in Villiers Street, Faustino Kiber of Ludiano was asked to pool all his tips. Rather than do so, despite an attempt at intimidation by some 'roffiani' [i.e. ruffians] employed by the manager, Faustino stormed out and refused to heed the manager's pleas to return.[101] Some 40 years later Giuseppe Giuliani, who was feeling off colour after a day off, got involved in a shouting match with the maître d'hôtel of the Royal Adelaide Gallery and also

walked out.[102] Similarly, and at about the same time, Luigi Togni left the café restaurant where he was working after 'a remark about my work made by Alfredo which was neither true nor fair'.[103]

A few must have had a hard time afterwards as one of the 'poor lads ... worn and shabby waiting in that long, pitiful black line of seedy applicants, now hopeful, now despairing of engagement outside the big London restaurants'.[104] If this was the case, however, they did not admit it to their more traditionally minded relatives in Switzerland, who had probably already been shocked at learning of their reckless defiance of the padroni. And in most cases, the waiters seem to have had no difficulty in finding employment elsewhere - even, like Faustino Kiber, in a restaurant owned by his former employer's nephews, Agostino and Stefano Gatti. The oral tradition of their descendants also suggests that waiters and chefs moved regularly between employers, bettering themselves in the process, like Bartolomeo Albertolli of Semione (1871 -1950). On his arrival in England, aged 14, in 1885, he worked at the prestigious Café Royal in Regent's Street, London. He then moved on to Gatti's and Monico's before opening a restaurant at 46 Chandos Street, Covent Garden with his older brother Battista, apparently in 1888/9. This closed after a couple of years, upon which he took work at Genoni's at Plymouth and then served as Chief Steward aboard a training ship of the Brazilian navy. After a year he had put aside enough in gold sovereigns to open another, longer lasting, café-restaurant of his own, with his brother, in Portsmouth.[105]

Some of the successful immigrants and former waiters or chefs who became restaurateurs eventually brought their wives and families over to England. They nevertheless often still sent at least some of their children to grow up with relatives in Switzerland. They may not have had time to look after them properly and did not want the children causing excessive noise in their flats above the restaurant.[106] More positively, they did not want their children to lose contact with their roots. Others left their wives and children in Switzerland.[107] In most cases it led to split families. On the positive side, it helped to maintain links with the home valley long after the father (or grandfather) of the family had emigrated to England. It ensured that well into the 20th century, the descendants of the waiters continued to marry girls from the Val di Blenio or the Valle Leventina and to maintain homes there. On the less positive side, it also meant some brothers and sisters who were separated from each other for years in wartime had different passports and could not talk to one another when they did meet.[108]

5. The earliest Unione Ticinese grave, Kensal Green Roman Catholic Cemetery, photographed prior to maintenance work in 1994.

The spread of the Ticinese 'Confectioner' 1847-1900

The expansion of Ticinese cafés in Britain after 1850 was phenomenal. The directories of the time, having no category for restaurant or café, listed them under 'confectioners and pastrycooks', but there is little doubt that, in this case, it meant café as well as confectioner's shop. Only a couple of confectioners with Italian names are to be found in London directories before 1848 when Carlo Gatti put in his first appearance.[109] The number hardly grew until 1854, by which time only Giuseppe Gatti (first recorded 1853), Natale Ferrario[110] and Antonio Brentini[111] (1854) had been added. From then, however, there was a steep rise, probably reflecting the Gattis' increasing prosperity and ability to rent small shops for their compatriots. In 1855 alone the d'Alessandri,[112] Marioni[113] and Rodesino[114] families, who were to continue to feature for decades, made their first appearance. By 1860, the number of 'confectioners' with distinctive Ticinese names had risen to 20 and by 1864 to 46.[115] Many were registered as having several premises. The Marionis (presumably relatives of Carlo Gatti's first wife Maria Marioni, whom he had married in 1839) had no less than 17 in 1860, of which Giuseppe Marioni ran 12.[116] By 1874, the year in which the Unione Ticinese was founded, the number of confectioners with Ticinese surnames had reached 62, again with several people owning a number of establishments. In comparison with the total number of registered 'confectioners' in the London area, the percentage was still relatively small. Nevertheless, the Ticinesi now formed the largest group after the native-born British confectioners - most of whom did not run cafés - and their number continued to grow. By 1880 there were at least 88 confectioners, café owners and restaurateurs in central London with Ticinese surnames.

The first cafés were to be found around the Italian quarter of London in Holborn, in the City, eastwards along Whitechapel and near the Strand and its continuation westwards, Fleet Street. In the course of the 1850s, the Ticinesi spread to Oxford Street, Tottenham Court Road, and the Euston Road. Oxford Street was, then as now, a major middle-class shopping area, though rather poor at the east end near St. Giles and Tottenham Court Road. Euston Road was then full of small shops, but was far from distinguished. Neither were the other major roads in which most of the early cafés and confectioner's shops were to be found: Edgware Road, Pentonville Road, Aldgate, Whitechapel, Bishopsgate, Shoreditch and Hackney High Streets. All these came to have numerous cafés and confectioner's shops run by Ticinesi (fig. 6). Camden High Street, Upper Street in Islington, Holloway Road , Borough High Street in Southwark and Westminster Bridge Road in Lambeth on the south side of the Thames also had several Ticinese establishments and were at best lower-middle-class. They were all relatively busy roads which attracted trade from locals and from visitors to the capital.

Some Ticinese properties began to be found in better-class areas from the late 1850s. Pietro De Giorgi (De Giorgi, Torriani & Co.) was briefly registered as a chocolate manufacturer at Titchborne Street near Piccadilly Circus in 1857-8. Domenico Marioni had a confectioner's shop in the same street in 1859 and from that year Giuseppe Marioni had a café at 221 Piccadilly, perhaps the most elegant street in London. The next decade saw the Brunettis opening in Pont Street in Kensington, the d'Alessandris in St George's Place, the Divianis in Crawford Street and the Marionis, again, in Knightsbridge, south of Hyde Park. However, these well-located establishments were a minority of the total number of Ticinese businesses. The 1870s saw the establishment of Pagani's Restaurant in Great Portland Street near Oxford Circus, Torriani Brothers in Brompton Road, Brentini's in Kensington High Street and, in a class of their own, from 1877, Monico's near and eventually (following redevelopment of the area) directly on Piccadilly Circus at the heart of imperial London.[117]

Isolated Ticinese establishments had begun to appear outside London from as early as the 1850s. An advert in the 1875 edition of Percy Butcher's *Cardiff Directory* for Giuseppe Gatti's Hotel du Continent at 158-9 Bute Street, Cardiff confirms that the hotel, 'one of the first class and most comfortable foreign hotels in Cardiff for Captains and Travellers'[118] was also a café and restaurant. Perhaps because of its location in the cosmopolitan docks area of Cardiff, it offered 'excellent cooking - French, Italian and English . . . Coffee in the French Fashion, Billiards, Newspapers in French, Italian and English'. It seems to have been modelled on the Gatti establishments in London, and was even, in its cuisine, ahead of them.

By the time the hotel is last recorded in 1894-5,[119] Ticinese cafés, confectioner's shops, tea rooms and restaurants had become familiar throughout the United Kingdom. From the mid-1870s Ticinesi had opened their own cafés in the better-class suburbs of London such as Wimbledon (Genoni), Putney (Togni), Croydon (Genoni-Pazzi) and Richmond (Ferrari, Valchera). It was a similar story in the resort towns along the South Coast of England. Margate (Torriani & Sons), Ramsgate (Bassi, Gatti), Eastbourne (Zanetti), Brighton (Gallizia, Biucchi, Bolla, Bontà, Lanfranchi), Littlehampton (Arrigoni), Southsea (Celeste Ferrari), Worthing (Ferrari-Togni), Hastings (Ferrari, Canuto, Cima), Bognor (Delmonico), Bexhill (Ferrario), Southampton (Ferrari-Jacomelli), Folkestone (Maestrani), Plymouth (Genoni), Bournemouth (Guidotti), Portsmouth (Albertolli) and Ryde, Isle of Wight (Albertolli) all boasted one or more Swiss café-restaurants.

They were also to be found in less fashionable, but increasingly populous areas. In several of the outlying

6. Early café-restaurants at 4 and 7 Aldgate in about 1880. Like many early examples Marco Polli's businesses were housed in old, once-grand premises. Note the advert for Gatti's chocolates which until 1873 had been produced a few doors away at 13 Aldgate. Aldgate is a relatively short street but in addition to these two establishments, it also boasted Monico & Bianchetti's at no. 23 and Monico & Mentasti's (later Guidotti's) at no.28. No.4 had previously been one of the numerous café-restaurants run by Giuseppe Marioni and the Gattis had also had a confectioner's at no.18 from 1856 to 1860. This density is typical of the early café-restaurants and suggests how popular they became. [By courtesy of the Guildhall Library]

districts that were being transformed into lower-middle-class London suburbs in these years, such as Finsbury Park (Pazzi) and Woolwich (Pedretti), Ticinese cafés were in the vanguard of urbanisation. Provincial towns, such as Chatham (Veglio), Northampton (Marchesi & Sons), Leeds (Jacomelli) and Colchester (Togni) also had their Swiss cafés or café-restaurants.[120]

Some of the proprietors, like the Bollas, Biucchis or Gallizias of Brighton, the Torrianis of Margate, the Veglios of Chatham, and the Jacomellis of Southampton, Bristol and Leeds, belonged to families that had opened cafés or pastry shops in London in the 1850s and 1860s,[121] or, like the Albertollis of Portsmouth or the Cimas of Hastings, they had begun their careers as waiters in London restaurants. So numerous were they that eventually it was to be said that there was not a South Coast town that did not have its Ticinese 'Swiss café'. By 1900, the Ticinesi had spread even farther -

going as far as Glasgow in Scotland (Francesco and Luigi Ferrari of Ludiano).[122]

Nevertheless, most Ticinese cafés were still to be found in the poorer districts of London and particularly in the vicinity of the major London stations. The Reggioris had café restaurants (founded in 1879 and 1883 respectively)[123] opposite King's Cross/St Pancras and Edgware Road Stations. Carlo Gatti's Café Restaurant de la Confédération Suisse and his nephews' Royal Adelaide Gallery were in the immediate vicinity of the newly built Charing Cross Station, while Odone's was close to Victoria Station. In 1890 a London guidebook disdainfully mentioned that 'In almost every thoroughfare in and out of London, the city and suburbs alike, [the Italian restaurateur] may be found plying his trade of cheap confectionery, chocolate, ices, lemonade, in some instances fair Italian wines, and tolerable cookery'.[124]

Three patterns can be discerned in the establishment and development of the 'Swiss café-restaurant'. In the first, the establishment remained in the hands of the same family and at the same address throughout its history. The most notable examples were the Royal Adelaide Gallery and Monico's restaurant on Piccadilly and Shaftesbury Avenue, which were owned by the Gatti and Monico families throughout their histories.[125] The same was true of many other establishments. Odone's at 152 Victoria Street passed from Giuseppe (recorded 1891/2-1916)[126] to Mrs. Florence Odone (1917-1919) to Otto Odone (1920-1) and Joseph Odone (1922/3-1936). Ferrari's Restaurant at Hastings (1885-1939) and, between 1921 and 1963, the other Ferrari restaurant (The Adelphi) at 10-14 Sauchiehall Street in Glasgow were also always owned by the Ferraris of Semione and Ludiano respectively.[127] The cafés of the Cimas, also of Hastings, and of the Albertollis of Portsmouth and Ryde, Isle of Wight, similarly never passed out of the hands of their founding families.

The second pattern is that of one family spreading from one café-restaurant to several, often in different towns. If the Marionis, Brentinis, de Marias, d'Alessandris, Gattis and Pazzis (Croydon and Finsbury Park) provide examples for London, the Ferraris of Semione in Hastings, Worthing, London (where a member owned a sandwich bar) and Tunbridge Wells and the Jacomellis of London, Southampton, Bristol and Leeds provide examples for the country as a whole.

These two patterns were more widespread than might appear at first glance, since shops sometimes passed through the female line or were acquired for sons-in-law with different names. In the context of the Gattis this included the Gianella, Biucchi, Corazza, De Bolla, Marioni, Andreazzi and Peduzzi families alone.[128] Other families with such links were the Brentini/Taddei and Gianelli (who successively owned 502 Oxford Street and separately owned several other restaurants), the Albertolli/Ferrari and Delmonico families (all of Semione), and the Taddei/Brentini/Diviani families of Campello in the Leventina.[129] More recent family networks, still represented in the Unione Ticinese, include the Togni/Pazzi/Genoni/Jacomelli/Diviani/Berti/Poglia and the Diviani/Cima/Bozzini/De Maria/Pedretti/Darani/Allegranza/Bonetti groups.[130]

The third pattern was that of the single restaurant which passed through the hands of several, unrelated Ticinese families. The most famous was Pagani's, which passed through two unrelated branches of the Pagani family[131] before, in 1903, coming into the ownership of Carlo Meschini of Magadino on Lago Maggiore, who had originally been the manager for Giuseppe Pagani. Another was Valchera's Restaurant in Richmond, which was bought from the Valchera family by the Jacomellis in the early 1920s.[132]

For most Ticinesi the acquisition and running of a café or café-restaurant was an expensive business, even with the assistance provided - at a price - by the Gattis. Many found themselves forced to go into partnership with their compatriots to survive. Judging from the entries in the London directories these partnerships were almost always short-lived, but most seem to have achieved their objective. Each of the partners survived, with his own premises, and with one of them usually at the old address.

Cafés into Restaurants ca. 1857-1900

Given the common social and family background of their owners, it is not surprising that the Ticinese establishments, large and small, bore a certain resemblance to each other. An informed contemporary felt able to talk of the Swiss café 'in its generic sense'.[133] Many cafés openly proclaimed their association with the Gattis on their fascias, claiming to be 'from Gattis' or even, in the case of Ferrari Brothers' restaurant in Hastings, 'Gattis'.[134] There may have been some legal necessity for doing so originally, because of the financial support the owners had received at the start from the Gattis. Nevertheless it soon became tantamount to a mark of quality. By 1887 a relatively independent guide to London, Charles Pascoe's The London of Today, considered that 'the most popular restaurant in London is 'Gatti's' in Adelaide Street'.[135] Agostino and Stefano Gatti eventually found themselves compelled to take action in face of the widespread, unauthorised use of their family name by other restaurateurs. They announced in the programmes of the Adelphi and the Vaudeville theatres that 'Owing to numerous misunderstandings A & S Gatti beg to state that the only Restaurants under their control are the Adelaide Gallery and the Adelphi'.[136]

The Ticinese establishments were not born as the restaurants or café-restaurants that they became. Many started as confectioners' shops with light refreshment facilities. They sold chocolates, lemonade, ices and pastries at the front and had a few round marble tables with red velvet seats, surrounded by large plate-glass mirrors crammed into the rear where customers could be served. This was the case with the confectioners' at 54 Great Portland Street that Mario Pagani took over from Pietro Torriano in 1871.[137] Others began as proper cafés which were 'accommodating imitations of the grander, more ornate and spacious cafés of the Continent, which were in some sort copied by the elder Gatti when he first entered upon business'.[138] While some chauvinist contemporaries sneered,[139] the more tolerant later fondly remembered 'the days of the old Hungerford Market Café and the worthy five fiddlers who nightly fiddled selections from Tancredi and the Italian masters, the while the customer sipped his chocolate or coffee. The fare provided was good, wholesome and cheap'.[140] The same source later noted that 'that café orchestra was the first introduced in London. It has been copied of recent years by almost all our leading West End restaurants and hotels. The elder Gatti helped Englishmen to their present appreciation of the Continental style of living more than any man of his calling.'[141]

Initially this was how Agostino and Stefano Gatti ran the Royal Adelaide Gallery. They themselves stated as late as March 1878 that until recently they had been operating as a 'Café and Refreshment Room for the supply of Tea, Coffee, Chocolate, Ices and other light refreshments'.[142] The accommodation on the first floor of the Adelaide Gallery consisted largely of small iron-legged marble-topped tables with the by now customary red velvet settees and mirrors.[143] The tables were not very different from those that were still in service at Pedretti's café at the Elephant and Castle, South London, in the 1930s.[144] Ladies were welcome - a considerable novelty at that time[145] - smoking was permitted[146] and chess and draughts could be played. With the 'French rolls, the Italian waiters and the cosmopolitan crowd' it seemed to the more adventurous young Englishman 'the nearest thing in the world to being on a honeymoon in Paris.'[147]

Many Ticinese establishments remained cafés to the end. In the late 1850s, however, the earliest restaurants to cater for the middle classes began to appear in London.[148] Some Ticinese cafés were among them. Carlo Gatti's establishments began serving 'chops and chips' in the Hungerford Market, and the latest fascias of Gatti & Bolla at 129 Holborn Hill unambiguously describe the business as a 'café-restaurant'.[149] The development was doubtless partly due to middle-class pressure, expressed in journals such as *The Builder*, for decorous and moderately-priced eating-quarters, envisaged as a middle-class equivalent of the Pall Mall gentlemen's clubs.[150] That Ticinese cafés were among the pioneers of this new style of eating, however, is probably due to the reputation that they already enjoyed for relative elegance, sobriety and moderate prices and to the direct pressure exerted by their impatient - and hungry - middle-class customers to improve still further. This was certainly the case with Agostino and Stefano Gatti's café. In their application for a wine and spirits licence in 1878 the brothers explained how by the mid-1870s 'in conformity with the wishes of the Frequenters of the Gallery' they had began to supply 'for the purpose of Luncheons Dinners and Suppers in addition to . . . light refreshments, Chops Steaks and other refreshments of a more substantial nature than previously'. By 1878 their customers were crying out for 'Beer and Wine to be drunk on the Premises with such Refreshments'.[151]

Contrary to what might have been expected, therefore, the Gattis and, by implication, their compatriots did not set out to create foreign-style restaurants for the notoriously conservative middle classes or to introduce them to continental cuisine. It was rather the reverse. Having created restaurants in response to popular demand, the Ticinesi, keeping their own opinion of the food to themselves, served the traditional English fare that their customers felt at home with. Charles Pascoe probably had the Royal Adelaide Gallery in mind when in the mid-1880s he wrote:

The man of taste . . . will find an abundance of gilding, tasteful woodwork, mirrors, coloured windows, decorated walls and ceilings, and the like; but five times out of six his choice of a dinner will be limited to one or two kinds of soup, possibly a couple of kinds of fish and the joint. An Englishman never tires of these served in the orthodox English fashion. The soup is usually not very tasty, the fish is plain boiled or fried, the joint is plain boiled or roasted. The last is generally the most satisfactory part of the dinner, and most moderate, even though hungry, Londoners content themselves with "the joint". And, if we may be permitted a word of advice in a friendly way, we would counsel those having the advantages of a good appetite to do the same'.[152]

When the Royal Adelaide Gallery was expanded and modernised in 1882 after the acquisition of a frontage to the Strand, the café was retained, turning the Adelaide Gallery into a genuinely hybrid café-restaurant.[153]

Once again the Gattis set the pattern which the other Ticinesi followed. The change is mirrored in the pages of Kelly's Post Office Directories. The number of Ticinese establishments to be found under 'Refreshment Rooms', a category first introduced in the 1862 edition, grew very slowly at first. It mushroomed from the later 1880s, with 'restaurants' gradually being added to the description. Many of the older Ticinese establishments evolved into restaurants, and several later immigrants were able to open restaurants as soon as they set themselves up independently in business, like the Albertollis. In the same years the number of Ticinese 'confectioners' in London gradually declined, though the overall number of 'Confectioners' also markedly increased, reflecting the growth in London's population and its rapidly improving standard of living. Yet many Ticinese establishments never rose beyond the level of café/confectioner and there was downwards as well as upwards pressure. Some 'cafés' eventually became sandwich bars or tea rooms, though still calling themselves 'Swiss café-restaurants'[154] (fig. 7, p 16).

The earliest surviving photographs of medium-sized Ticinesi establishments date from the 1880s. They all have the same plate-glass shop fronts with little to distinguish them externally from the other shops in the row.[155] As often as not Gattis' together with the owner's name is to be seen on the fascia. White lettering on the windows advertises the soups, fish, chops and steaks 'from the grill',[156] coffee, teas, ices, beers and Gatti's chocolates that were available at moderate prices. The crowded shelves on view contain the sole concession to foreign taste - a few bottles of wine and, particularly, flasks of Chianti (fig. 8, p 17).

By the early 1880s, however, change was slowly coming to the English palate. Charles Pascoe caught the mood with his comments that 'Continental customs in dining are . . . taking the place in London of the old "ros-bif" style. Potatoes are seldom seen in their jackets now. They are served *à la Lyonnaise*. Mutton cutlets are served *à la Francais*, and so on; but neither, we think is the better for the change'.[157] Again the Gattis began to adapt to this new taste and by 1889 Pascoe was recording that 'a good many undergraduates in gastronomy confound the Anglo-French with the French dinner. The first may be had for half-a-crown any afternoon at Gatti's in the Strand. The second is only to be had in London by paying well. . . '.[158] Pascoe might sneer that 'the only 'illusions' the majority of us care to cultivate are those which by the substitution of a French for an English name, turn a reputable English dish into a disreputable French one'.[159] Most Ticinese restaurateurs were only too happy to pander to this illusion. It satisfied the increasing vanity of the ambitious, lower middle-class clerks, who formed a large part of their clientele outside the West End of London,[160] brought no challenge to their essentially conservative English stomachs and filled the coffers of the restaurant owners quite satisfactorily.

A few years later Pascoe was writing of the 'Anglo-Swiss-French' style of cooking to be found at the Adelaide Gallery.[161] But the Gattis had already begun to expand from this style to a more genuinely French one - with correspondingly higher prices for the authentic French dishes.[162] Not that the essentially English menu was sacrificed. The new dishes were simply grafted onto the existing menu as that had earlier been grafted onto the original café's simple bill of fare.

In the early 1900s, small restaurants in the South Coast resorts, like the Albertolli brothers' restaurants in Portsmouth and Ryde on the Isle of Wight, still served essentially English fare. Even on grander occasions, such as Armistice Night in the 1920s, the cuisine was basically English though the menu was printed in French.[163]

The heyday of the Swiss Café-Restaurant 1900-1930

In 1885, Charles Pascoe wrote that 'As to prices, a hungry man may satisfy his appetite in reasonable comfort for 2s 6d; a fastidious man for a trifle more, say 5s; a diner who can show good play with knife and fork upon fish, flesh and fowl and whose pint of claret makes but a poor account on the bill for 7s 6d; an epicure for 10s.'[164] A year later, in the next edition of his guide to London, the lowest price was raised to 3s 6d. By 1900 this was unchanged. The price for a superb, genuinely French meal, had, however, risen to £1 at a time when there were 25 Swiss francs to the £ (as compared to about two today). This provides a standard against which to judge the value for money, and class, of the Ticinese café-restaurants.

An elaborate nine-course banquet at Reggiori's large restaurant facing King's Cross Station cost 5s 6d per head in 1897.[165] The restaurant correspondent of the respected *Pall Mall Gazette*, Lieutenant-Colonel Newnham-Davis, recorded in 1899 that a rather extravagant meal for two, with a bottle of good wine, liqueurs and coffee, at the much more fashionable Monico's Restaurant cost £1 12s 6d. The main element of this, the eleven-course table d'hôte meal, however, only cost 5 shillings per head. A similar meal at Pagani's, including two pints of Veuve Clicquot, cost £1 13s 2d, but the ten-course à la carte meal, which was a little less extravagant than that at Monico's, cost 7s 10d per head. By contrast, a simple but substantial two-course table d'hôte meal at the Adelaide Gallery cost the Colonel 3s. 9d. He considered this a good example of how, at Gattis, 'one could get a large amount of good food at a very easy tariff'.[166] Pascoe advised his readers that in most Italian-Swiss restaurants 'one may dine - a chop, steak, or plate of meat with vegetables - . . . for 1s. 6d. to 2s.'[167]

The large, purpose-built and more prestigious

7. Two waiters, the young Savino Cima and his relative Carlo Vanzetti, both of Dangio, stand in front of Costante Torriani and Sons' *Little Swiss Café Restaurant* at 22 Marine Drive, Margate in about 1910. Little more than a confectioner's (though it was linked to larger establishments in Margate and London), Torrianis, which was in operation from 1879 until the later 1930s, stood at the opposite end of the scale from grand London establishments such as Monico's. Yet they shared a common ethos, interior decor and personnel. [Collection of the late Natale Cima]

8. Carlo Menegalli, his wife and staff (probably family) in front of their café-restaurant at 87 Tottenham Court Road in about 1885. Menegallli, whose business is recorded at this address from 1882 to 1900, had received loans from the Gattis as is alluded to, with some pride, on the fascia. Note the wide variety of (mainly English) fare on offer and the bottles of Chianti in the window [Casagrande archive, Bellinzona].

restaurants offered more for the money one paid. In addition to a generally superior quality of chef, the locations were fashionable, the eating areas more spacious and the architectural pretensions grander, with the extensive use of marble in the case of Monico's.[168] Almost all seemed to have a grand dining room that could be used for banquets on the first floor, with somewhat smaller, more select suites or dining rooms, including a ladies' room, around it. There was usually a string orchestra (of differing sizes), always a café area that did its main business during the daytime, a grill room and sometimes a beer hall and a billiards room.[169] Monico's, the Royal Adelaide Gallery and the Gatti brothers' other establishment, the Adelphi Restaurant, were known for their pre-theatre dinners.

Beyond that, each had points of individuality. The Royal Adelaide Gallery was distinguished by the continued presence in the dining rooms, despite the enormous wealth they had accumulated from their business and theatrical activities, of Agostino and Stefano Gatti. They were always to be found at a well-placed oval table 'between the long gallery with its clothless tables and the aristocratic end of the restaurant . . . to which each waiter brought every dish that was to be served, and there was a mysterious exchange of what looked like metal tokens'.[170] The exercise was primarily intended to reduce the possibility of fraud on the waiters' part, but it gave a reassuring impression of attention to quality. In terms of public relations it also compensated for the 'bustle and clatter' which visitors repeatedly complained about and which was caused by the numerous waiters removing plates and cutlery from their metal trays, by customers walking on the carpetless stone floors and by the echoes of chatting and merry-making in the cavernous halls of the restaurant.[171]

Monico's had been grandly rebuilt in 1888-9 following the enlargement of Piccadilly Circus, onto which it now found itself facing, though its principal entrance was in Shaftesbury Avenue.[172] Pascoe considered it one of the best places in London to get a proper French meal. It was 'a good dining or luncheon place conducted in good style after the continental manner' where 'at midday and the dinner-hours you will find no inconsiderable proportion of the better class of foreigners - French, Italian, Swiss and others - co-mingling'.[173] It was particularly well known for its Winter Garden, the sumptuousness of its decor, which abounded in marble, fancy plasterwork, mirrors and miniature palms (*cover*), and its numerous suites. These included Renaissance and Louis XIV suites, but perhaps the best-known was the Masonic suite, designed in Egyptian fashion in 1914, on the second floor.[174] It continued to be famous for its style and quality until the Second World War, and the corner of Piccadilly Circus and Shaftesbury Avenue that it dominated was long known as 'Monico's Corner'.

Pagani's, which had opened in Great Portland Street in 1871, was, by contrast, recognised as early as 1890 as

a distinctively Italian restaurant (fig. 9). By 1901 it was considered 'quite the best' of them, 'though somewhat Bohemian'[175] and distinctly 'romantic' in atmosphere.[176]

It gained this reputation in part from its handsome 'Venetian' Art Nouveau tiled and mosaic façade, the lower part created in 1874 by Charles Werley and the more spectacular upper part in 1901 by Beresford Pite.[177]

The restaurant's romantic aura stemmed mainly, however, from the famous Artists' Room on the second floor. At no more than 8 feet (about 2.7 metres) square and with space for only one table it was small. But it was reserved for the owner's special guests and from 1874 they had been encouraged to sign their names, sometimes with a message or a caricature, on the brown wallpaper. By the 1890s these signatures, drawings and caricatures, amounting to some 5000, had been mounted onto panels which were interspersed with portraits of the relevant well-known artists, composers, authors, singers, actors and actresses (fig. 10). The signatures continued to grow in number over the following decades, ultimately covering fourteen panels in all.[178]

Thirteen of the original fourteen panels containing over 5000 signatures still survive, having been removed from the walls for safe-keeping in 1939. The signatures include a wide range of celebrities between the 1870s and 1950s: not only actresses (e.g. Sarah Bernhardt, Lillie Langtry, Fay Compton, Evelyn Laye), actors (Henry Irving), singers (Caruso, Maurice Chevalier, Nellie Melba), music-hall stars (George Robey), composers (Tchaikovsky, Puccini, Mascagni, Leoncavallo, Luigi Denza, Arnold Bax) and conductors (Toscanini, Henry Wood), but also writers (Oscar Wilde, Stefan Zweig, George Grossmith, H.G.Wells), artists (Whistler), cartoonists (Carlo Pellegrini, Phil May, Bruce Bairnsfather) and even television personalities (Annette Mills and Muffin the Mule).

Pietro and Luigi Reggiori had their main restaurant at 1-3 Euston Road, opposite King's Cross Station. Founded in 1879, its rather humble street frontages onto Euston Road and Liverpool (now Birkenhead) Street gave little indication of the splendours that lay within. By the later 1890s it had expanded into the former King's Cross Theatre and was capable of accommodating about 250 diners at one time and 800-900 people in the course of a day. The luxuriousness of its surroundings bore comparison with Monico's, the walls and numerous pillars being embellished with decorative ceramic work (Burmantofts faience), plentiful mirrors, enormous stained-glass 'cathedral' windows, and a fountain in the middle of the main dining room (*see back cover*). The menu was extensive and lavish, though French names usually concealed essentially English dishes. The speciality of the restaurant, however, seems to have been its breakfasts, with as many as 200 breakfasts being served daily before 7 am to cater for the passengers who poured off night-trains coming from the North.[179]

The humbler Swiss café-restaurants could not hope to compete with this, though many tried to. The general resemblance of their interiors was unmistakable. All, at least in their later forms, had the same 'meretricious decorations, . . . pink and green glasses, . . . silver grid-irons, . . . slabs of plated ware [and] windows of coloured glass' mocked in the 1880s by Pascoe.[180] Some, like the Pazzi and Genoni families' Café Royal in Croydon, which had begun life as a confectioner's in 1874, followed Pagani's in having their fronts remodelled in elegant Art Nouveau style shortly after converting themselves into restaurants.[181] White linen-covered tables with silver(ed) cutlery, sharply folded linen napkins and silver cruets surmounted by a carnation or a candle lined the walls of the long, narrow ground-floor dining rooms of many of the smaller restaurants. At the rear of the room, and beyond the subdivision if there was one, a small wooden staircase led up to

TELEGRAMS: "SOUFFLE, LONDON." TELEPHONE No. 2710, GERRARD.

Pagani's

PART OF THE GRAND RESTAURANT

CORNER OF THE GRAND RESTAURANT PARISIEN

THE MAIN ENTRANCE

THE KING'S ROOM

THE ARTISTS' ROOM

"Ben faranno i Pagani."
PURGATORIO, CANTO XIV.—DANTE

9. A menu from Pagani's of about 1925, featuring photographs of the elegant exterior and interior, including the Artists' Room [Meschini family archive, Magadino].

a further dining room on the first floor. At least in the earlier part of the 20th century, this was reserved for women. Reggiori's café-restaurant in Chapel Street facing Edgware Road Station in 1897[182] and Valchera's in Richmond in the 1980s were laid out in this manner.

Despite attempts to trade on their similarities, these lesser establishments could not offer the sumptuous luxury of Monico's, Pagani's or Reggiori's. Like the Royal Adelaide Gallery, however, they could provide wholesome food and good service in pleasant surroundings at very reasonable prices. This reputation, supported by regular advertisements in their local press, was sufficient to keep most of them in business well into the 20th century.

The Ticinese Englishman in Ticino

In 1873 Giovanni Veglio (b. 1831) of Corzoneso in the Val di Blenio applied for naturalisation as a British subject. A 'Confectioner and Restaurant Keeper', he lived with his wife and young daughters Adelina and Virginia above the café-restaurant at 314-316 Euston Road that he had been running since 1868. He had probably arrived in England in the 1850s when his family opened their first London cafés, and earlier in the 1860s he had been proprietor of a café at 102 Park Street (now Parkway), Camden Town. He had applied for British citizenship, he stated, 'from a desire to pursue my Business avocation, from a wish to improve the [business] connection I have already formed and from a desire to become the possessor of freehold and other landed property within the United Kingdom in order to secure to myself an honorable independence or at least a sufficiency for my after years whilst my Business is prosperous and I am in good health'.[183] These good, practical reasons for British citizenship did not preclude a continuing attachment to Ticino or a growing affection for Britain. To this day members of the Veglio family, though British subjects for over a century,

continue to foster their links with Switzerland. From an early date this mingling of British and Ticinese loyalties and affections also had repercussions inside Ticino.

A waiter, on his return to Switzerland, was likely to continue to support his English football club[184] and, as the surviving letters show, to pepper his Italian with English words such as 'bara' (bar), 'manidger' (manager), or 'cians' (chance). Similarly, in his book *Alps and Sanctuaries*, published in 1881, which first popularised the Ticinese valleys among the British, Samuel Butler wrote that

'I have rarely sketched in villages [in the Val di Blenio or the Valle Leventina] without being accosted sooner or later by some one who could speak English, either with an American accent or without. It is curious at some out-of-the-way place high up among the mountains to see a lot of children at play, and to hear one of them shout out, "Marietta, if you do that again, I'll go and tell mother"'.[185]

The English influence extended into their homes. Another English tourist of the time described with amusement mixed with horror how she met 'a pleasant, rosy-cheeked youth, just over twenty, recently returned from a two years' service in London to . . .a little Swiss inn' in Ticino. "I have learned a few things in England", . . . [he] said to me "Yes, I have learned something very fine". And he drew my attention to the quaint white-

10. One of the artists' panels from Pagani's, this one (unlike most) including a portrait but also the signatures of George Gershwin (composer), Eugene Goossens (oboeist) and Evelyn Laye (musical comedy actress) amongst many others. [Courtesy of Sotheby's, who own the copyright]

washed walls of the inn, made hideous by Japanese fans and cheap paper rosettes, &c. . . . "Ah, I shall do this place up in fine style," he said, looking contemptuously round him at the modest but picturesque paternal inn. "Why, you will hardly know it again next year! I shall have the salle-à-manger pypered - (he had learned the cockney dialect well) "pypered with bunches of fruit, flowers, monkeys - all in the English manner - ah! you will see! I shall wake them all up!'[186]

The Ferrari family displayed their lasting nostalgia for Southampton, their English home, in a related but more spectacular fashion. To this day their villa in Semione is adorned by a tower with neo-gothic windows recalling those of the Bargate, a medieval town gate in Southampton, next to which their successful café-restaurant was situated.[187]

These villas were and remain the most visible relics of the prosperity of the successful Ticinese emigrants to Britain. Generally containing two or more floors, they occupy a prominent position above or along the principal road through their home village. Most conform to the standard design for the villas of prosperous late 19th-century emigrants, which are to be found throughout Ticino and not only in the Val di Blenio or the Leventina. They are multi-bayed. The central, circular doorway has a stone surround and a small balcony immediately above. Corridors run like spines through the centres of the interiors to stone staircases in the rear. The exteriors often conceal or concealed spectacular painted interiors, like that still surviving in one of the Ferrari houses in Semione. Its colourful *salone* on the first floor is adorned with neo-rococo painted walls and ceilings containing vignette alpine landscapes. In these the careful observer will note telegraph poles - a silent tribute to the creed of progress. Other villas were specially designed and

architecturally much more ambitious, with dramatic skylines containing numerous eaves.

Carlo Gatti and (separately from him) his brothers Giuseppe and Giovanni built large, conventional villas annexed to their more humble birthplace in Marogno near Dongio, in the Val di Blenio. In 1897, while still busily working in London, Giuseppe Pagani built a handsome villa, named 'Villa Lina' after his wife, on the site of his birthplace in Torre.[188] The Odones, though they were from Bellinzona, built themselves a villa at Olivone at the top of the valley. Semione, near the bottom, contained the villas of several branches of the Ferrari family, while Ludiano was graced with the villa of the Ferraris who had established themselves in Glasgow. The d'Alessandri family, who had café-restaurants in Oxford Street and at several other addresses in the elegant West End of London, built a large home for themselves at Primadengo in the Valle Leventina. The Meschini family, the proprietors of Pagani's from 1903, owned a palatial villa, which had formerly been a hotel, in their home village of Magadino. Its painted interiors built around an internal courtyard look out over Lago Maggiore, and its grounds originally extended to its shores.[189]

Almost as conspicuous as the houses are the tombs of the successful emigrants. Carlo Gatti's still grandiose tomb in Bellinzona, with portrait bust and carved allegorical mourners, the symbolism of which reflects his descendants' pride in his honesty and success as an ice-importer rather than as a café owner,[190] was originally even more imposing. The tomb of the Gattis' associates of the 1850s and 1860s, the Monicos, contains carved busts and portrait plaques of the senior members of the family. It dominates the little graveyard at Dongio, marginalising the more modest graves of Giuseppe and Giovanni Gatti and their wives.

These Ticinesi did not wait until retirement before making their presence felt in their home canton. Carlo Gatti managed to return to Ticino for most summers between 1829 and 1848 when he was living in relative penury in Paris,[191] and retained regular contact

11. The Cima-Norma chocolate factory at Dangio portrayed in naive style in about 1930. The factory is now closed, but old customs die hard: a present-day descendant of Giuseppe Pagani, who created the building, is married to a Swiss descendant of Agostino Gatti.

afterwards. In 1867 he was elected to the *Gran Consiglio* of Ticino to represent the Circolo di Malvaglia in the conservative interest. In doing so he was following in the footsteps of his older brother Giuseppe who had sat on the Gran Consiglio between 1844 and 1852, the same years in which, despite his long absences in Paris, he had also served as mayor of Dongio.[192] Carlo remained a cantonal councillor until 1875.[193] Nor was he inactive, though he preferred not to speak from the floor of the chamber.

Before Carlo's death his nephew Agostino had advanced one level higher on the political ladder, representing Ticino on the Federal Council in Bern from 1873 to 1893.[194] Stefano also took an interest in the stormy world of Ticinese politics and served on the Ticinese *Gran Consiglio* as representative for the Distretto di Blenio from 1875 to 1893.[195] Where Carlo was staunchly liberal and anti-clerical after 1871, his pious nephews remained firmly conservative.[196] Neither played an active part in Bern or Bellinzona and hardly ever spoke, though they attended sittings of the respective assemblies whenever business in London allowed (usually in June and December).[197] But it was not for their political skills that they had been adopted as candidates. If their repeated re-elections could in part be attributed to the traditional influence and local standing of their patrician family, their success in England was probably a more important consideration. Carlo Gatti, at least, must have thought so since he had an article lauding his achievements in London, which had first appeared in *The Chimney Corner* of 17 December 1870, translated into Italian for his election campaign of 1871.[198] As for Agostino and Stefano, it was rumoured that the brothers owed their high standing with the conservative political élite to their ability as late as the 1890s to transport their waiters and other compatriots from London to Ticino to vote for conservative candidates at cantonal and general elections.[199]

Carlo Gatti, however, was far from being the only Ticinese in London to support the liberals and radicals, and in the 1880s and 1890s the Ticinese community in Britain was riven by the violent political divisions that affected their home canton. Pietro Pazzi, the proprietor of a café-restaurant at Finsbury Park Gates, was as deeply wedded to the radical cause as Agostino and Stefano Gatti were to the conservative-clerical. In September 1890 Pazzi was involved in aiding and then facilitating the escape to England of a fellow radical, Angelo Castioni, after he had assassinated a young conservative Ticinese politician in the course of a failed attempt to overturn by force the conservative Ticinese government (which included Agostino Gatti's brother-in-law). Swiss attempts to secure Castioni and Pazzi's extraditions ended in failure (in the process, embedding the principle of the inviolability of political asylum in English law) but the Swiss national, cantonal and local authorities deprived Pazzi of citizenship and he was never again able to return to his homeland.[200]

The 'British' Ticinesi also made positive marks on their home canton. The cantonal archives in Bellinzona contain a series of letters from Carlo Gatti dating from the early 1870s addressed from his iceworks in New Wharf Road or his office at the Concert Hall and Billiard Saloons in Villiers Street. They show him subscribing the enormous sum of £2000 towards the construction of a carriage road over the Lukmanier, offering to provide capital for the whole project at 4.5% interest and then following its progress.[201] The transfer of a total of £10,000 (worth approximately £380,000 today) from his account at Coutts in London to the Banca Cantonale

in Bellinzona between 1875 and 1877 suggests that he made good his offer.[202] Further money was invested in projects intended to benefit Ticino, such as the experimental farms established at Gudo, Sementina and Moleno.[203]

Giuseppe Pagani used part of the money from the sale of his Great Portland Street restaurant in 1903 to assist in financing the building of a railway from Biasca to Aquarossa. Opened in 1911 it was - a sign of the times - intended as much to bring tourists into the Val di Blenio as to transport young Bleniesi out.[204] Partly with the same intention of encouraging local employment, Giuseppe Pagani took over and enormously enlarged a chocolate factory in Dangio in 1915. Within a few decades 'Cima-Norma' had about 200 employees[205] (fig. 11). In a less spectacular way a former waiter at Gatti's, Giuseppe Cusi, who later became a successful bookmaker, founded a home for handicapped children at Olivone. This still continues, though in a new building. Through their contributions to the Unione Ticinese, the smaller confectioners and waiters also contributed to the welfare of their home canton. In its very first year, 1874, the committee of the society decided to send £10 or 250 francs to those who had suffered in the floods of the 15 August of that year. Three years later a total of £45 or 1125 francs was sent to assist the victims of the great fire that had destroyed Airolo, and the tradition continued for as long as Ticino was poor enough to need help from abroad.[206]

The end of the story 1930-1987

The Swiss Café-Restaurant, in its differing manifestations, continued to flourish for two and sometimes even three generations. The 1930s, however, saw the start of a gradual decline, with the number of closures for the first time not being surpassed by the number of new enterprises that opened. Odone's at 152 Victoria Street, London, closed shortly before 1936, as, about this time, did Torrianis in Margate.[207] The first of the great restaurants to go was the Royal Adelaide Gallery, which closed in 1939.[208] Pagani's struggled on into the mid-1950s, and at the end of that decade Monico's was sold to Forte.[209] In 1963 Ferrari's Restaurant in 10-14 Sauchiechall St in Glasgow passed out of the family's hands and closed a few years later. Reggiori's in the Euston Road also disappeared in this period after a lengthy period of decline. In 1987 the Jacomelli family sold 'Valchera's' in Richmond, apparently the last of the Swiss Café-Restaurants in Ticinese hands, and it disappeared shortly afterwards.[210]

There were several causes for the decline. The first was undoubtedly a failure to respond to changing tastes in popular eating after 1920. The café-restaurants that closed in the 1970s and 1980s and the tea and refreshment rooms that closed in the 1930s were still recognisably the same in terms of décor as those of 80 and 90 years earlier, though the menus had become distinctly more continental. No concession was made to the mass-produced culture of the Lyons Corner House, the 1950s espresso bar, the hamburger establishments of the 1960s or McDonalds and the fast-food chains of the 1980s. This was, however, what the general public increasingly wanted, and the Ticinese restaurateurs neither would nor could compete in terms of décor - or price. At the more expensive end of the market there was a proliferation of restaurants offering specific national cuisines, particularly Italian and French, whose menus left the Swiss Café-Restaurants lacking a distinctive profile.[211] Where the restaurants did succeed in maintaining a profile, based on a high-quality 'international' menu and the traditional Swiss décor, service and style, as at 'Valchera's' at Richmond, they continued to flourish despite charging higher prices and catering for a wealthier class of customer.[212]

A second factor, which perhaps also contributed to this loss of clear profile, was the drying up of emigration after 1905 as a result of increasingly severe British immigration controls. It became more and more difficult to sell restaurants on to compatriots who had recently arrived in England, as had frequently been the pattern before 1900. Ticinese waiters were also harder to find. In restaurants which employed family members the effects took some decades to be felt. By 1934, however, it was becoming noticeable.[213] By the 1970s, Switzerland's refusal to join the European Economic Community had almost totally halted immigration and prevented all but the most exceptional Swiss chefs from finding employment in Great Britain.

A third factor can best be described as personal, institutional or political bad luck. Personal tragedies frequently brought restaurants to the point of closure. The loss of her four young 'angioletti' broke the heart of Ida Odone of Odone's Restaurant in Victoria Street, who died in 1904 aged 38. Her husband, Giuseppe, died while still in middle age a decade later.[214] Their restaurant managed to struggle on. But the death of two young children from diphtheria was sufficient to lead Elvezio Ferrari of Semione, under pressure from his wife, to close their restaurant in Tunbridge Wells and to return to Switzerland.[215] In 1947 the death of Agostino Berti and his son from a gas leak led to the closure of their restaurant in Stroud Green Road near Finsbury Park in North London. The early death of Francesco Allegranza in 1933, leaving a daughter and an unborn son but no adult Ticinese able to carry on the business which he had been running with Roberto Belgeri of Dongio, and the bleak economic climate, forced the closure of his café in Worship Street in the City of London.[216] Disasters came in less personal forms. Compulsory purchase for redevelopment caused the closure of the Cima family's café at White Rock in Hastings in 1932 (the site is now covered by a bus station)[217] and the Albertolli family's 'Continental' restaurant in Portsmouth in 1973.[218] The wartime legislation forbidding aliens to reside more than 20 miles from London is said to have led to the closure of Ferrari's restaurant in Hastings at the start of the Second World War.[219] Bombing claimed several others: large ones, like Pagani's which never really recovered from its bombing in 1940, and smaller ones like Rodolfo and Santino Pedretti's café near the Elephant and Castle which succumbed in 1942 and their cousins, the Daranis', café in New Cross which was destroyed in 1944.[220] Fate could also be kind. Many - possibly the majority - of the

12. Sir John Gatti in the 1920s: very much the suave Englishman. In his hand, however, he holds a 'Brissago' cigar, recognisable from its shape, manufactured in Ticino. The family's account at Coutts show repeated payments for them by Sir John. [Peduzzi archive]

more successful restaurateurs like the Pagani, the Meschini, and the Monicos, eventually returned to Ticino where several opened restaurants.[221] From 1960 increasing prosperity inside Ticino and particularly the growth of the tourist trade made emigration unnecessary and Britain less attractive to young Ticinesi even had there been no impediments on the British side.

But all the while, many of those who remained in Britain had been gradually loosening their links with Ticino. Absence from home brought independence from the restrictions of Ticinese life. In 1911 Giuseppe Giuliani assured his aunt and cousins that, apart from them, he did not miss Ticino. Since being in London he had not been to church and could do without 'the trumpetings of Master Curate against emigration'.[222] Others found themselves falling in love and marrying English girls. As early as 1884 Luigi Togni informed his mother that 'Today at 9 a.m. I married Miss Cecilia Legg, a young English girl. . . She's not beautiful or rich, but to balance that she's a good worker and a better economist than me . . . As for me, dear mother, don't worry a bit: being married to a young English girl rather than a Swiss or French girl won't make any difference: I'll still be your son.'[223] He added that he would continue to 'help you with advice and money and everything that you need', but the die had been cast. He and his descendants remained in England.[224]

Before about 1925 it was generally regarded as a misfortune to die in England, and whenever possible an additional memorial stone was erected in Ticino. The short verse on Pietro Reggiori's tombstone of 1907 in Kensal Green Cemetery contains a nostalgic mention of the 'elvetici monti' ('Swiss mountains') from which he had been exiled during his working life; there is a memorial stone to him and to his wife Monica in Lottigna. The memorial stone in Castro for Virginia Debolla, who died in London in 1891 aged 43, contains the number of her burial plot in Kensal Green. As late as 1926 the body of Ernesto Rodesino was transferred to Ticino, though there is also a mention of him on a Unione Ticinese monument in Kensal Green. In 1897, however, Agostino Gatti was buried at Kensal Green in a grandiose tomb, to be joined there in 1906 by his brother Stefano. Though this resembles their father Giovanni's tomb in Dongio, there is no additional monument to them in Ticino. Battista and Bartolomeo Albertolli are commemorated in Semione but buried in Portsmouth. Bartolomeo's wife, Stefanina, actually died in Semione in 1956 but decreed that her body be transferred to Portsmouth for burial.

Inevitably, increasing assimilation and prosperity were loosening the links with Ticino and the café and restaurant trade. The process was most clearly illustrated in the case of Agostino Gatti's oldest son (fig. 12). He was born in Dongio in 1872 and Italian was spoken at home.[225] His father had been naturalised as a British subject before his birth, however, and where Agostino had been active in Swiss politics, a public career in Great Britain was open to John Maria. His education was typical of that of the sons of well-to-do British families of his generation. He boarded at a leading Roman Catholic public school, Stonyhurst,[226] before going up to St. John's College, Oxford.[227] He was called to the bar at the Inner Temple in 1894, though he had little time to practise before taking over his father's business in 1897, and in 1897 he married an Anglo-Welsh girl, Lily (d.1964), the daughter of Dr Samuel Lloyd. While dutifully pursuing his business interests in electricity and entertainment, he devoted his energies to a political career in London. From at least 1906, he was politically active as a

councillor and alderman on Westminster Council within whose jurisdiction his theatres, restaurants and the offices of his electricity supply company lay, and he served as Mayor of Westminster in 1911-12. In 1918 he was elected to the London County Council and began to play a role of national significance. Between 1920 and 1927 he was Chairman of the Finance Committee, which had extensive powers over the lives of about 8 million Londoners - as much as the total population of Switzerland. In 1927-8 he served as Chairman of the LCC, or in effect as mayor of most of London outside the business quarter of the City. It was for these services that he was knighted in June 1928. Like his father, John Gatti was politically a Conservative.[228] Like him he was sociable. But where Agostino was always to be found in the Royal Adelaide Gallery, John had little to do with it.[229] Instead, he was a member of two London gentlemens' clubs: a Conservative club, the Constitutional, and, appropriately for the owner of two theatres, the Garrick, a club where actors, writers and intellectuals could mix. His wife was a poet[230] and he himself was 'a dilettante in literature and art, a collector of rare books, prints and book-bindings.'[231] He described himself as being of a practical bent and listed his recreations as mechanical work and golf. It was on the golf course near his country home in Littlestone in Kent that he suffered a fatal heart attack in September 1929.[232] Contemporaries thought that 'there is some suggestion of Italy about him, though he is a most patriotic Englishman'[233] and his family continued to be in contact with the Ticino well into the 1970s - his sister Maria and one of his daughters, Joan, died there while visiting their cousins in the Val di Blenio in 1951 and 1971.[234] Nevertheless, John and Rocco had surrendered their family property in Dongio as early as 1911[235] and there could scarcely have been a more British life than Sir John's.

Many other Ticinese restaurateurs apart from the Gattis did well enough to enable their children to avoid the rigours of the catering life. Of those who remained in Britain, some have gone into the media or have become architects and teachers. Others, like the former England goalkeeper, Peter Bonetti, whose family used to run a café-restaurant in Putney High Street, became sports stars. In all cases their family restaurants have passed into history. It is only through the Ticino Bakery Ltd of Bermondsey Street, London, which is owned by the Gianelli family from Faido, formerly owners of a chocolate factory and two café-restaurants in Oxford Street, that the Ticinese catering tradition in Great Britain has continued into the late 1990s.

But before getting too nostalgic one should recall the reality of their ancestors' lives whether they were owners of small café-restaurants, chefs or waiters. During a rare free moment at Gatti and Rodesano's restaurant at 166 Strand, on 21 August 1886, Colombano de Giovannini penned the following bitter words to his brother who was thinking of emigrating from Olivone in the Val di Blenio to Nice:

'Here in London now there's nothing good to report. The bosses treat their staff worse by the day . . . there's nothing new about leaving home: bad food, worse sleep and then working like a donkey and earning little. If you'd had my experiences, you wouldn't even try to make your way in the world.' [236]

Acknowledgements

The authors would like to thank numerous friends and colleagues for their assistance, and particularly the late Vittorio Abate, Frank and Albina Allegranza, the Albertolli-Holland family, the late Virgil Berti, Joe Bonetti, Joe Broggini, Serse Cima, Gemma De Maria, Annetta Diviani, Fausto Ferrari of Glasgow/ Ludiano, Fernando Ferrari (Corzoneso), Raffaella Ferrari (Semione and Zurich), William Gatti (great-grandson of Agostino Gatti), Pino Gianelli, Frances Meschini (Magadino), Joe Pedretti, Joe A. Piffaretti, Mrs Federica Veroli-Piazza-Frishman (a great-great-granddaughter of Carlo Gatti) and Bunny Veglio. They also wish to thank the staffs of the cantonal archives in Bellinzona, the Greater London Record Office, the National Monuments Record (London), Ralph Hyde and John Fisher of the Guildhall Library, and particularly Barbara Peters and Tracy Earl, successively archivists at Coutts Bank who allowed them to consult the bank's ledgers at the outhouse in East London and at the Bank - on the site of the Gattis' *Royal Adelaide Gallery* - itself.

All originally Italian quotations in the text and the following notes that are taken from published sources have been rendered in English translation alone. Where the sources are not published, the original Italian is given in addition to the English translation.

Notes to the text

1 Charles Eyre Pascoe, *London of Today.* [1901 edition] (London: Sampson Low, Searle, & Rivington, 1900), p.137. In the 1903 edition (p.118) the same author commented that 'cafés, under various fanciful names, now permeate every district of London, both City and West End, not to add central and suburban'.

2 *Kelly's Directory: Marylebone, 1900-1901.* They were Veglio's (no.17), Stefano de Maria (35), Charles Guidi (45), d'Alessandri Swiss Café (36, 393), Vanoni & Tinelli (171), Luigi Taddei (502). There were other restaurants run by Italians at 432 (Antonio Bisacca) and 526 (Onorato Angelinetto).

3 Raffaelo Ceschi, 'Bleniesi Milanesi. Note sull'emigrazione di mestieri dalla Svizzera Italiana' in *Col bastone e la bisaccia per le strade d'Europa. Migrazioni stagionali di mestiere dall'arco alpino nei secoli XVI-XVIII* (Bellinzona: Edizioni Salvioni, 1991), pp. 59-61. The figures for the Valle Leventina related to the villages that were higher up on the mountain slopes and distant from the Gotthard Road. Those closer to the Gotthard Road offered greater employment possibilities.

4 Federico Bruni, *I Cioccolatieri. Dall'Artigianato all'Industria* (Bellinzona: S.A.Grassi & C., 1946) particularly pp. 20, 29-75. The first edition of *Murray's Handbook for Travellers in Switzerland* (London: John Murray & Son, 1838), p.197 also commented that 'many of the chocolate-sellers and chestnut-roasters, who swarm in the streets of the cities of Italy, come from the Val Blegno'.

5 For the 'chain' nature of migration in the Italian community, see Terri Colpi, *The Italian Factor: The Italian Community in Great Britain* (Edinburgh: Mainstream, 1991), pp. 33-4, 53.

6 Ceschi, pp. 66-7. Ferdinando Cesare Farra and Giuseppe Gallizia, 'L'Emigrazione dalla Val Blenio a Milano attraverso i Secoli' in *Archivio Storico Lombardo* 1961, pp. 117-130. Rich emigré individuals could afford more: the founder of the Collegio Papio in Ascona, one of the leading schools in Ticino, in the late 16th century, Gregorio Papio, was an Asconese merchant resident in Rome.

7 Terri Colpi, pp. 34-37.

8 Ceschi, pp. 67-71.

9 Ceschi, p.61.

10 Gianni Berla, 'Migranti ticinesi a Parigi (1830-1850)', *Archivio Storico Ticinese,* xxviii (1991), p.106.

11 Felicity Kinross, *Coffee and Ices. The Story of Carlo Gatti in London* (Lavenham, 1991), p.12.

12 Kinross, pp. 10-11.

13 Berla, p.131; Pino Peduzzi, *Pioneri Ticinesi in Inghilterra. La Saga della Famiglia Gatti 1780-1980* (Bellinzona: Casagrande, 1985) pp. 49, 166; Kinross, p.11 (Righenizi & Gatti); Peter Jacomelli archive. Information from Annetta Diviani née Morosi, whose uncle ran a business in Lyon.

14 The table in Ceschi p. 60 shows that in August 1847 only 8 males from the Val di Blenio were in London (but nowhere else in the British Isles) out of a total of 366 emigrés of military age in a total population of military age of 835. Berla discovered from the Swiss consular records that between 1830 and 1850, 157 Ticinesi emigrated from Paris to London. The vast majority of these were glaziers from the Leventina or labourers from the Mendrisiotto (Berla, p.119). When Carlo Gatti arrived in Dover in 1847, he classified himself as a 'mechanic' (Kinross, p.12) and he later said he had worked, *inter alia*, as a glazier in Paris (*Chimney Corner*, 17 December 1870, p. 25). So presumably the Leventinese glaziers who arrived in England may eventually have turned their hands to other types of work.

15 Ceschi, pp. 66-7.

16 Ceschi, pp.59.

17 Berla quotes one *marronaio*, Giuseppe Bontà, writing to Carlo Guidotti from Boulogne as early as the winter of 1838/9, that 'In the new year I'll close down my place, because I'm making nothing, and I'll be off to London' (p.131). Berla's figures also show that the residence permits granted to Ticinesi and the Swiss in general declined dramatically between 1841 and 1851: from 220 permits in 1833 and 230 again in 1853 down to 21 in 1844, 15 in 1848, 16 in 1850 and never more than 71 (1843) throughout the decade (p.102). As late as October 1860, Stefano Protti of Grumo wrote from Paris that he was intending to leave for London to work for Giuseppe Gatti as a *cioccolatiere* 'seeing that here in Paris there was no work' [Sonia Fiorini, 'Lettere di emigranti bleniesi in Inghilterra', *Archivio Storico Ticinese* xxix/111 (1992), pp.151-2].

18 Gianni Berla, p. 144. There was nothing new in this xenophobia. The Holland-Albertolli family possess a letter of 29 August 1830 from Paris describing the revolution and mentioning that 'The Swiss are despised. We're being asked questions every day. They want us all to get out of the country' ['I Svizzeri . . . sono mal veduti. Abbiamo tutti i giorni questioni. Volevano che se ne vadino tutti fuori dello Stato'].

19 There is plentiful evidence among the family papers of the older 'London' Ticinese families for their French background and continuing links with France. The heirs of the late Bart (Elvezio) Albertolli own the passport of his great-grandfather (b.1799) for travel to Paris in 1831, and several letters of the 1860s to Pietro Genoni of Semione, 'marchan de Marons faubourg du Temple, Paris'. The ledgers of Coutts Bank show Giuseppe Gatti in London still doing business in Paris in October 1861 (Carlo Gatti's account) and Agostino and Stefano Gatti transferring £400 to their relatives, the Righenzi, in Paris in 1880. Even as late as the 1890s, a grandson of Giuseppe Gatti, Giuseppe Peduzzi, was sent to work at the fruit importing business of his cousins Appollinari et Righenzi in Paris (Peduzzi, p. 58) At a humbler level, Peter Jacomelli's archive contains correspondence with Paris stretching from 1850 to 1876 in the form of correspondence addressed to Guidotti and Guidotti et fils, chestnut merchants at Strasbourg and Mulhouse (October and November 1850) and a postcard from Pietro Pazzi, a restaurateur of Seven Sisters Road, Finsbury Park (North London) to Battista Togni, a *marronaio* in Paris (1876).

20 The Alpine and Sub-Alpine regions were particularly well represented: David R.Green, 'Little Italy in Victorian London. Holborn's Italian Community', *Camden History Review* 15 (1988), 2-6. Colpi, pp. 36, 41-2, 44-5; Lucio Sponza, 'The Italians in London' in Nick Merriman (ed.), *The Peopling of London. Fifteen Thousand Years of Settlement from Overseas* (London: Museum of London, 1993), pp. 129, 132. The Unione Ticinese continued to make a donation to the Italian Hospital in Queen Square, London, founded in 1884, until the latter's closure in 1989 (for which see Colpi, pp. 64-5, 248-9).

21 Colpi, pp. 28-30. I am grateful to Tom Fattorini, whose family now own the largest private foundry/mint in England, for this information about his ancestor.

22 Kinross, p.12.

23 Kinross, pp. 11-13; *The Chimney Corner*, 17 December 1870, p.25 paints a slightly more positive picture. Peduzzi, p. 49.

24 *Oxford English Dictionary*.

25 Pascoe, *London of Today* (1885), pp. 43,48; Caroline Liddell & Robin Weir, *Ices. The Definitive Guide* (London: Grub Street, 1995), p. 13; see also *The Chimney Corner* , 17 December 1870, p.26: 'Most of us can remember the time when . . . an ice-cream . . . only came within the reach of the "bloated aristocrat"', and Charles Dickens jr, *Dickens's Dictionary of London* (London, 1880), pp.230-1: 'A very few years ago . . . a really good dinner was almost entirely confined to the regions of club-land, and, with one or two exceptions, respectable restaurants, to which a lady could be taken, may be said hardly to have existed at all'. In the 1827 edition of *Leigh's New Picture of London or, a view of the political, religious, medical, literary, municipal commercial and moral state of the British Metropolis* (London: Samuel Leigh, 1827), a well-established guide to the town, only two pages out of more than 500 are taken up with the listing of eating places. See also Donald J. Olsen, *The Growth of Victorian London* (London: Batsford, 1976), pp. 101-3, 108.

26 *Leigh's New Picture of London* p.377. The numbers are unlikely to have altered much before 1850. The first cafés and restaurants in railway stations only opened later.

27 Pascoe, (1885) pp. 44-5 echoing the words of Thomas Verity, the architect of the the Gaiety Restaurant on the Strand (1869) and the Criterion Restaurant on Piccadilly Circus (1874), in his talk on 'The Modern Restaurant' to the Royal Institute of British Architects in 1879 (*The Architect* xxi (1879), 30 quoted in Olsen, p.103). Pascoe (ibid.) also speaks of 'foreign establishments which dispensed their hospitalities . . . to crowds of strange men, wearing strange garments, and talking in strange tongues. Here . . . the study required an appreciation of foreign manners and customs, as well as of foreign tastes, not always to be found in the self-satisfied Briton'.

28 *Leigh's New Picture of London* (1827), p. 378.

29 *Chimney Corner*, p.26.. He could not have stayed there long since there is no record of him in the St Pancras Rate Books for the years 1847-1850. I am grateful to Malcolm Holmes of Camden Libraries for having searched on my behalf.

30 *Kelly's Post Office Directory* for 1848 records under 30 Great Hall, Hungerford Market, 'Gatty Chas, pastry cook'. Carlo would probably have had to be in occupation of the shop by the closing months of 1847 to be included. Kinross seems to have missed this entry. For Hungerford Market see Kinross, p. 18.

31 Kinross, pp. 15-16. Peduzzi (less accurately), p.118.

32 Kinross, p.15.

33 *Kelly's Post Office Directories* for London.

34 *Kelly's Post Office Directories*, 1849-1862.

35 They had arrived in London from Paris at some time between spring 1850 and 1852, spurred perhaps by their younger brother's success (Peduzzi, p.73, Kinross, p.21 cf. Berla p.131 n.82 who cites a document signed by Giuseppe in Paris on behalf of the family firm Gatti & Righenzi on 19 March 1850).

36 A corrective to the rather grand impression of *Gatti's-in-the-Road* to be gained from the illustration, from a programme cover, reproduced in Kinross, p.40 is to be found in a sad photograph showing the bombed-out building (by then *Gatti's Cinema*) in about 1947 held by the National Monuments Record (London).

37 In addition to *Kelly's Post Office Directories*, see *Chimney Corner* 17 December 1870, p.26 (which plays on his sentimental attachment to the site of the Hungerford Market); Kinross, pp.35, 39, 41-2 and Greater London Record Office, Middlesex Records, Music and Dance licences [MR/LMD/ 25/30, 25/47a, 16/1, 3/10]. Carlo Gatti's account at Coutts Bank (1857-78) suggests that the *Arches* brought in twice as much income as the *Palace of Varieties*.

38 Kinross, pp. 15, 25-34.

39 Peduzzi, p. 58.

40 *Kelly's Post Office Directory*, 1853, 1856. Peduzzi, p.58 (who wrongly states on p.118 that 18 Aldgate was owned by Carlo).

41 *Kelly's Post Office Directory*, 1855-6, 1858-60.

42 Peduzzi, pp. 49, 151. To put these music halls in context it should be recalled that by the early 1880s there were 408 music halls in London, under the jurisdiction of the Middlesex and Surrey magistrates, and that only *Gatti's-over-the Water* (Westminster Bridge Road) of the Gatti's music halls merited a mention in a reputable guide to London - and then only in passing (Pascoe, 1885, pp.90-91).

43 A Joseph Gatti is recorded in various *Cardiff Directories* as proprietor from at least 1858, and an advert in the 1875 Directory (p.44) speaks of the café-restaurant as having been established 16 years. In the 1861 census Carlo and 'Peppina' Gatti aged respectively 17 and 28, Joseph's son and daughter, are listed as the house's occupants. These are probably Giuseppe's children Carlo Domenico (1844-68) and Giuseppa (1831-1899) [family tree in Peduzzi, p. 34]. By 1875-6 'Mrs' Josephine Gatti is listed as the proprietor. Though Giuseppe had died in 1873 (being survived only by daughters), it could well have taken 18 months to two years for the inheritance formalities to be completed and for the change to be recorded in the Directory. Having no husband, unlike her sisters, Giuseppa would have needed an independent source of income, such as a hotel could have provided. It seems that as she got older, Giuseppa lied about her age: 28 (correctly) in 1861, she is 35 in 1871, 46 in 1881 and 54 (!) in 1891. Perhaps more telling is the mention in the 1881 census of a 16-year-old visitor to Cardiff, Josephine Peduzzi from Greenwich. In 1881 Giuseppa had a 16-year-old Peduzzi niece. She was a Martina (1865-1940) not a Josephine, but the entry may refer to her after all. Her Greenwich origins (given the Greenwich connections of Giuseppe Gatti) would suggest so. Moreover, the fact that *all* the women in 158-9 Bute Street in 1881 are named as Josephine implies a slapdash copyist. I am most grateful to Mr. Joe A. Piffaretti of Cardiff for supplying me with this information.

44 Census 1861 for Hungerford Market Upper Level.

45 Obituary of Stefano Gatti, *The Globe*, 13 October 1906 [archive of William Gatti]. *Baedeker's London and its Environs* (Leipzig: Karl Baedeker, 1866). According to family legend (Peduzzi, p.74; Kinross, p.39) the café was opened by their father Giovanni, who was also said to have been instrumental in promoting the first of the promenade concerts (see note 47). There is no evidence for this in the Post Office directories or in the ledgers of the Gatti accounts at Coutts Bank, but it must be likely that he was closely involved. The National Monuments Record has later photographs of the Adelaide Street frontage.

46 *Survey of London*, 31 (London: Survey of London Committee, 1963), *St James's Westminster* p.74. Obituary of Stefano Gatti, *The Evening Standard*, 12 October 1906 [archive of William Gatti]. Giacomo Monico set up his own establishment. For its later story see pp 17, 21.

47 Obituaries of Stefano Gatti in *The Evening Standard*, 12 October 1906, and *Daily Mail*, 14 October 1906. The ledgers of A & S Gatti's account at Coutts Bank for the 1870s show enormous sums of money flowing in from these concerts. These concerts may originally have been a development from the string bands which, in French style, played in Gatti cafés (see p. 14 below).

48 *Survey of London*, 36 (London: Survey of London Committee, 1970), *St. Paul's Covent Garden*, pp.243, 245. The *Adelphi* was initially leased and purchased only in 1881.

49 Peduzzi, p. 153.

50 Obituaries of Stefano Gatti from the archive of William Gatti. And cf. Olsen, p.104.

51 See p. 14.

52 Lieut.-Col Newnham-Davis, *Dinners and Diners. Where and How to Dine in London* (London: Grant Richards, 2nd ed., 1901), p. 374.

53 Olsen, pp. 104-8.

54 Pascoe, *London of Today* (1885), p. 51; Newnham-Davis, pp. 67-70; Anonymous magazine article describing the interior and function of the *Adelaide Gallery*, with several pen-and-ink sketches, datable to c.1882, in the Philip Norman collection, Guildhall Library.

55 R.H. Parsons, *Early Days of the Power Station Industry* (London, [1953?]), pp. 106-8. (Felicity Kinross archive, London Canal Museum). Peduzzi, pp. 93-103. William Gatti still possesses a length of the cable that was laid along The Strand in 1885, displayed in a glass case.

56 Peduzzi, p.74; Giuseppe Giuliani of Aquila to his parents, London 31 May 1908 (Fiorini, 'Lettere', p. 158 no. 14).

57 e.g. Onorato Boscacci and Giacomo Moresi, aged 42 and 37 recorded at 435 Shaftesbury Avenue in the 1891 census.

58 George R Sims, *Living London* (London: Cassell, 1903), iii, p.185: 'swarthy Swiss Italians, in blue and pink shirts, of the Val de Travers Company'.

59 The numerous icemen employed by Carlo Gatti were also predominantly Swiss, with a few Italians (see Kinross, p.60). However, Italians came to predominate under his daughter Rosa (1845-1927) and her Corazza descendants who were associated with the Parma region, even though they originated from Dongio (Peduzzi, pp. 138-145; Kinross, p.43).

60 *Chimney Corner* 17 December 1870. Carlo had the article translated into Italian and reprinted in the following month as part of his 1871 electoral campaign in Ticino. Since he is unlikely to have voluntarily exposed himself to potentially damaging public accusations of lying, it can be assumed that this was true. It also fits in with stories told by descendants of Ticinese restaurateurs, of him visiting these restaurants personally on his horse and cart to gather the rent. It could be that in the 1850s he acquired the cafés at 7 Edgware Road and at 254 Oxford Street for his countrymen rather than for himself: both were registered as cafés of Domenico Marioni, a kinsman of Carlo's first wife, by 1858 before passing, by 1860, to the Monico brothers - who were closely associated with other Gatti ventures at that time (*Kelly's Post Office Directories*).

61 Coutts Bank ledgers show a series of payments to Massimo and Pietro Pazzi in 1873 and 1874, £4000 to N. Cizzio on 4 November 1873 and a series of payments amounting to £281 to Agostino Berti in 1875. There are records of payments to individuals with distinctively Italian, non-Swiss names, suggesting that Carlo was also helping in the establishment of Italian caterers, whose numbers grew dramatically after 1880 (and see Colpi, pp. 52-64). The ledgers show that Carlo possessed lands in Italy (particularly along the Piedmontese shores of Lago Maggiore) from the 1850s and like most of his contemporaries he seems to have felt there was no contradiction in being a loyal Swiss from Ticino and being an enthusiastic Italian.

62 The ledgers of Carlo Gatti's account at Coutts Bank show that he paid small sums, often of only £10 or £12, to the Pettenatis (1861), Natale Ferrario (who owned numerous confectioners) (1862), G. Baretta, A. Brentini (both 1864), Bernasconi (1869), Cizzio and Pedretti (1870), and Trongi (1871). Note of repayment by Brentini suggests these were loans.

63 Peduzzi p.50 citing Giuseppe's account book, which apparently recorded loans of more than 100,000 Swiss francs (£4000) to Bleniesi restaurateurs.

64 Letterhead on a letter from Marco Ferrari to his father, 4 December 1876 [Jacomelli archive]. There is a photograph of the exterior of the establishment a couple of decades later, when it was operating as a café-restaurant as well as an ice merchant's, in John Cloake, *Richmond Past* (Barnet: Historical Publications, 1991), p.90 ill. 161.

65 Mrs E.T. Cook, *Highways and Byways in London* (London: Macmillan, 1902), p. 289 describing young Ticinese waiters in London.

66 Carlo Genoni to his parents, 30 July 1872: 'I had to work 6 months to pay my journey' ['ò (sic) do[v]uto lavorare 6 mesi per pagare mio viaggio.'] [Peter Jacomelli archive].

67 Carlo Bonetti et al., *Along a High Way of History. National Museum of the St. Gotthard* (Bellinzona: St Gotthard Foundation, 1989), pp. 106-113, 149-154; Andres Furger, *Der Gotthard-Postwagen* (Zurich: Schweizerisches Landesmuseum, 1990). *Murray's Handbook for Travellers in Switzerland* (1838), pp, 92-4; *Baedeker's Switzerland* (Leipzig: Carl Baedeker, 1881), pp. 125-6 ff.

68 The journey was still far from cheap. Atanasio Cima of Dangio to his parents, London, 15 April 1896 gives the total cost of his journey to London (Biasca to Basle; Basle to Paris; Paris to London) at 89 francs 50 centimes (£3/11/7d or £3.58), with the most expensive stretch being from Basle to Paris (Fiorini 'Lettere', p. 157 no. 12).

69 The membership of the Unione Ticinese (see p. 10) dramatically increased in the years around 1900 ([Oscar Gambazzi], *Sessant'Anni di Vita Ticinese a Londra. Breve rassegna storica in occasione del 60mo anniversario della sua Fondazione 1874-1934* (London: Unione ticinese, 1934), p. 6). Cf. the identical phenomenon with the Italian community, peaking in 1913, noted in Colpi, pp. 48-9, 54, 63. The growth took place in the provinces and in the London suburbs. And see p. 12.

70 25.2 years (1851); 25.3 years (1861); 22.8 years (1871); 21.14 years (1881).This is based on an analysis of the census returns 1851-1881 for Gatti properties published by Kinross. It is not as representative a sample as could be wished, giving a total of about 180, with a maximum of about 45 in 1881, out of a total Ticinese population in England that has been estimated, rather unscientifically, as having reached 2000 or more in 1900. In the absence of a wider documented sample, however, it has to suffice. 48 of this total of 180, or 29%, were aged between 18 and 20. The number grows to 84 or just over 50% if the 17-24 year-olds are isolated. The relative balance between the ages remains broadly similar in each of the censuses, though in each decade more Ticinesi are recorded. The chefs were consistently older, and generally in their mid- or late 30s.

71 As well as the slip of paper (fig. 4) Peter Jacomelli possesses an envelope of 1876 addressed to Carlo Genoni at Renters Farm, Carlo Gatti's farm in Hendon, north of London.

72 Young Ticinesi of good family, generally en route elsewhere, were invited to stay in the Gattis' private homes (Giovanni Pedrazzini to his parents, London 19 October 1877 in Piero Bianconi (ed.), *Lettere di Giovanni Pedrazzini dall'America ai Familiari* (Locarno: Pedrazzini, 1973), pp. 3-5).

73 Cook, p.288. There is a London Ticinese folk memory of lots of Ticinesi living in Newport Dwellings, Newport Place, one of the poorest streets in what was then a very poor area north of Leicester Square (information from Peter Jacomelli and Richard Tames, *Soho Past* (London: Historical Publications, 1994), p.79). There may be independent support for this in a survey of ethnic minorities in Soho undertaken in the 1890s which revealed 258 Swiss living in the area - 6% of the total number of foreigners and the fifth-largest minority after the Germans, French, Italians and Poles and larger than the Russians, Belgians, Swedes, Austrians, Dutch and Americans (Tames, p.41). It seems likely that most of these Swiss were Ticinese waiters.

74 Giuseppe Giuliani to his parents, 31 May 1908 (Fiorini, 'Lettere', p. 158 no. 14): 'I sleep together with Giovanni. In this house, including waiters and everyone, there are about 180 workers.' He was working at the Royal Adelaide Gallery (436 Strand). Given the paternalism of the Gattis, all 180 men were probably working there. In another letter (Fiorini, p.158-9 no.15) he repeats unambiguously 'At home I sleep with Giovanni di Cherlucin in the same bed'. For a graphic description of the Soho lodging houses, often sparsely-furnished, carpetless former mansions with partitioned rooms, where 'head-porters and waiters [were] the aristocracy' see George R. Sims, *Living London* (London: Cassells, 1903), i, p.243.

75 Fiorini, 'Lettere', p.158 no. 14.

76 Faustino Kiber to father. Adelaide Gallery, 18 March [c. 1875] (Fiorini, 'Lettere', p.150, no. 1). He seems to have been paid 40 francs (equivalent to £1 12s, or £1.60) for a whole year at a time when a meal in a good restaurant cost 25p (5 shillings) [*Dinners and Diners* (1897), introduction].

77 Though the surviving letters suggest that as time went on and the rate of emigration increased, most seem to have had uncles, cousins and even brothers in England.

78 eg Luigi Togni to a brother, 14 December 1915 in the middle of the First World War, when travel to Switzerland was all but impossible, 'Now all I miss is my wife' ('Ora non mi manca che la . . . moglie') [Peter Jacomelli archive].

79 eg 'I found the weather quite different from what it was in Semione [Val di Blenio]: cold and rainy and foggy', ' we have really sad weather - nothing but rain' ['ò trovatto la stagione tutte di ferente (sic.) da samione[,] fredo e piogée e nebiaso'; 'qui abbiammo un tempo triste sempra pioggia' [Orsola Ferrari to her mother, 7 July 1884 , July 1890]; Luigi Togni to brother-in-law, 27 January 1883: 'The weather is bad. It rains every day, and it's cold and windy, But I dare to hope that after the bad will come the good' ['La stagione è cattiva piove tutti i giorni freddo e vento ma oso sperare che dopo il cattivo verrà il bello'[Peter Jacomelli archive]. He was evidently an optimist.

80 Giuseppe Giuliani to his parents, 31 May 1908 [Fiorini, p.158, no.14].

81 Information from Joe Bonetti, Frank Allegranza, Joe

Pedretti, and Peter Jacomelli, whose father was manager of such an establishment, at Earlsfield in South London, early in his career. It seems there were enough Ticinesi and Italians to support such social centres, which would have had to rely exclusively on Ticinese and Italian custom and (as the ledgers of Coutts Bank reveal) occasional subventions from Agostino and Stefano Gatti.

82 Colpi, p.60; Sims, i, p.243. Significantly, Sims distinguishes between Italians, Swiss and Ticinesi as though the latter formed a distinct category: possibly a reflection of the number and visibility of Ticinesi in London by 1902 and of Sims's own friendship with Agostino and Stefano Gatti. He had written melodramas for the Adelphi in the 1880s and was to attend Stefano's funeral in 1906 [see obituaries and accounts of the funeral in the archive of William Gatti].

83 Peduzzi, p. 89. Stefano was well known for his sweet nature and unostentatious philanthropy, but as of February 1874 his motives may have been partly political: the years 1873-1875 marked the beginnings of Agostino's and Stefano's political careers in Switzerland (see p. 21). Because of a misprint in the history of the Society produced on its centennial in 1974 (p. 2) Peduzzi gives the initial membership as 1010. In fact it was 101 (the list of original members still survives and is published by Kinross, pp. 61-2).

84 Protti, who started as a worker in Giuseppe Gatti's chocolate factory, is listed in the Post Office Directory for 1865 only as running refreshments rooms at 2 Old Compton Street, Soho. For letters of Protti, who came from Grumo in the Val di Blenio, see Fiorini, 'Lettere', pp. 151-2, letters 3, 4.

85 1881 census in Kinross.

86 1871 census in Kinross. The ledgers of Coutts Bank show numerous payments to both men by Stefano and Agostino Gatti and by Carlo Gatti and his daughter Rosa Corazza, indicating how much the different branches of the family relied on them.

87 Information from Peter Jacomelli, more than confirmed by the surviving photos and tickets for the functions.

88 Coutts Bank ledgers, Agostino and Stefano Gatti, 2 May 1881.

89 Giacomo Degrussa of Olivone to his brothers, London 8 March 1888 (Fiorini, 'Lettere', p. 156, no. 10) seems to be referring to it in the case of his friend Ambrogio who had been ill with bronchitis. The Unione Ticinese only finally abandoned provision for this in 1995, though it had become largely irrelevant after the creation of the National Health Service in 1948.

90 [Oscar Gambazzi], *Sessant'anni di Vita Ticinese a Londra. Breve rassegna storica in occasione del 60mo anniversario della sua Fondazione 1874-1934* (London: Unione Ticinese, 1934), p.5. The minute reads that the Hospital would accept "any sick members on condition that there was space, the hospital would not undertake to leave a bed free for the Society, because this would cost £60' ('qualsiasi socio ammalato colla riserva se havvi posto, non rendendosi l'ospedale responsabile di tenere dei letti appositamente per la Società, perchè il tenere un letto apposta costerebbe sessanta lire sterline.'). The Hospital was then situated in Agar Street, off the Strand, only a few steps away from Gatti's Royal Adelaide Gallery (436 Strand).

91 Gambazzzi, p. 4. Eventually three other plots were purchased. After 1945 five more plots were purchased in the St Pancras Cemetry in Finchley. These are still being used for members. The ages of the ten members commemorated on the oldest headstone, who died between 1878 and 1892, ranged from 32 to 54 with an average age of 41.8 at time of death - a reflection of the hard life led by many of them. Since most waiters were in their twenties, few of those commemorated are likely to have been waiters at the time of their deaths, though they may have started their careers as such. Luca Rodesino (1832-1888) had been a confectioner (i.e. the owner of a small café) at 73 Regent's Park Road, Camden Town (*Post Office Directory: London, 1874*). He could probably have paid for his own grave. As a founder member of the Unione Ticinese, however, he may have chosen to be buried in the Society's grave out of a sense of solidarity.

92 Cook (n.65), pp. 287, 289.

93 eg 'And if I knew how to speak English I could already have had a job earning £1 a week. But, as far as English is concerned, I know sweet all.' (Guadenzio Cima of Dangio

to his brother, London 18 December 1899; Fiorini, 'Lettere', p.157, no. 13). Few of the waiters probably learned much English because of the lack of contact with English speakers outside their work. One of the advantages cited by Giuseppe Giuliani about his new job in Manchester was that it gave him 'lots of chances of learning English well because we are sleeping at an English family's' [to his parents, 22 November 1910] (Fiorini, 'Lettere', p. 159, no. 16)

94 Luigi Jacomelli to his brother, Southampton, 6 July 1916 [Peter Jacomelli archive]; Giuseppe Giuliani of Aquila to cousins, n.d. [c.1908] (Fiorini, 'Lettere', p.158, no.15)

95 Giovanni Genoni to his sister-in-law, 4 March 1894; 'Tognina' (Antonina Pazzi) to her cousin, Croydon, 5 December 1932, (who wanted to clear her taxes 'so as not to lose my rights in case I return there with my children' ('onde non perdere i diritti se per caso vengo in paese con i miei figli') [Peter Jacomelli archive].

96 Giovanni Togni to Ida Togni, Bexhill, 2 March 1908 [Peter Jacomelli archive].

97 Giuseppe [Togni?] to his brother 21 December [1897?]; Marco Ferrari to his father, 4 December 1876 [Peter Jacomelli archive]; Colombiano de Giovannini of Olivone to his brother, London 10 June, 21 August 1886; Giacomo Degrussa of Olivone to his brother, 8 March 1888 (Fiorini, 'Lettere', p. 154-5, 156, nos. 7, 8, 10)

98 Marco Ferrari to his father, 4 December 1876; Luigi [Togni?] to brother, London, 14 December 1915 [Peter Jacomelli archive]; Stefano Protti to mother and sister, Paris 28 October 1860 (Fiorini, 'Lettere', p.151 no.3)

99 Giacomo Degrussa of Olivone to his brother, 2 August 1886 [Fiorini, 'Lettere', p.155 no. 9].

100 Fiorini, p. 148. Domenico Giuliani to his wife, London 5 January 1883 (Fiorini, p.153, no. 5). Fiorini assumes that the 'consigliere' referred to is Agostino Gatti, but it was Stefano, a cantonal councillor, who suffered the worse health (see for example, his obituary in *The Referee*, 14 October 1906), though he outlived his brother.

101 Faustino Kiber to his father, Adelaide Gallery, 18 March [c.1870] (Fiorini, 'Lettere', p. 150 no. 1).

102 Giuseppe Giuliani to his parents, Manchester, 27 November 1910: 'I hurled abuse at him right in the middle of the dining room and then I stormed straight out' (Fiorini, 'Lettere', p.159, no. 16).

103 'un rimarco fattomi da Alfredo sopra il mio lavoro, non essendo vero ne giusto'. Luigi Togni to a brother (?), 16 Hereford Street, Edgware Road, London, 1 November 1916 [Peter Jacomelli archive].

104 Cook, p.289.

105 Information from his son, the late B.E.(Elvezio) Albertolli in letters to J. Pedretti and P. Barber, 2 February 1982, 29 January 1985. Also *Post Office Directory* (London), 1889, 1890, 1891.

106 This was, for example, the experience of Peter Jacomelli and his siblings whose parents ran restaurants in Wimbledon and then Richmond.

107 This occurred with the Ferrari family of Semione, who had a restaurant in Hastings (and later elsewhere). Information from Raffaella Ferrari. Other families seem to have tried to ensure that their children were born in Ticino. Elvezio Albertolli, whose father had a restaurant in Portsmouth, was brought to England from Semione aged 9 months in 1907 (his letter to J. Pedretti, 2 February 1982). Agostino Gatti's oldest son, the later Sir John Gatti, was born in Dongio in 1872, though the descendants of his great-uncle Carlo Gatti made a point of being born in England (see Kinross, p. 34).

108 Several members of the Unione Ticinese still fall into these categories.

109 As Felicity Kinross points out, *Kelly's Post Office Directories* for London were always one year out of date and sometimes a couple and even more: Veglio's restaurants of Euston Road, Oxford St and Tottenham Court Road recorded their foundation year as 1855 on their menus (I am grateful to Mr Serse Cima for allowing me to see the example that he owns), but 'Veglio Charles & Co 431 Oxford St and 17 Tottenham Court Road' is first recorded in the *Directory* only in 1858.

110 At 103 Holborn.

111 At 95 Whitechapel Road.

112 10 Black Prince Row, Walworth Road, South London (later to be taken over by the Jacomelli and, by 1866, by the Carati families).

113 4 Pleasant Row, Pentonville

114 14 Bishopsgate Without, City.

115 The number of Italians with non-Ticinese names registered as confectioners grew until about 1858, after which it remained steady and even diminished slightly. Presumably the *padroni* of these Italians lacked the wealth and energy of the Gattis.

116 As of 1860 people with distinctive Ticinese names ran 39 premises in central London; as of 1864, 63. The sudden increase after 1860 may be a belated reflection of the Austrian blockade of Ticino and expulsion of the Ticinesi from Lombardy a few years earlier.

117 This was owned by Agostino and Stefano Gatti's former partner Giacomo Monico.

118 Butcher's *Cardiff Directory* (1875 edition), p. 44.

119 I am grateful to Mr Joe A. Piffaretti of Cardiff for uncovering this information and allowing me to utilise it here.

120 These names are derived from personal information, confirmed from the relevant directories.

121 For instance, the Gattis who ran a restaurant in Ramsgate seem to have been cousins of Carlo's branch of the family and possibly related to the Agostino associated with Carlo at Hungerford Market in the 1850s and the Gattis who later ran Gatti & Rodesino at 66 The Strand.

122 *Kelly's Post Office Directory* Scotland, 1900 (under *Glasgow*, which had no less than 5 Ferrari-run establishments: *The Globe* (West Nile St) and *The Adelphi* (Sauchiehall St, named after Agostino and Stefano Gatti's second restaurant on the Strand) being the grandest.

123 'The Development of the Swiss Café in London. A Visit to Reggiori's Restaurants'. *The Caterer and Hotel-Keepers' Gazette*, 16 August 1897, pp. 436, 438.

124 Pascoe (1890), p.72.

125 *Survey of London* vol. 31 (1961), p.74.

126 His tombstone in Olivone, however, states that he died in 1914 - another example of the outdatedness of Directories.

127 The *Adelphi*, by then known as *Ferrari's Restaurant*, passed out of the hands of the Ferrari family between 1963 and its final closure a few years later.

128 See genealogical tables in Peduzzi and Kinross and cf. the names given in the Post Office directories.

129 The Brentini and Diviani families continued to intermarry into the middle of the 20th century.

130 This paragraph is largely based on information from Joe Bonetti. Other Unione Ticinese members provided numerous important facts about their relationships.

131 For Giuseppe Pagani (1859-1940) of the second line of Paganis to own the restaurant, see Bruni, *Cioccolatieri*, pp. 71-2.

132 Valchera's briefly passed out of Ticinese hands after 1987 before its final closure in the early 1990s.

133 *Development of the Swiss Café*, p. 434. He wrote, in clarification: 'There are ... Swiss cafés and cafés which, ... with a Swiss basis, are practically cosmopolitan in character. Of all of these . . . there are distinctive grades . . . but the majority of these are either good - some very good indeed - or . . . good to middling'.

134 Photograph of ca. 1900 in the possession of Peter Jacomelli reproduced in Peduzzi, p.155.

135 Pascoe, *London of Today* 1887 edition, p. 51.

136 And cf. 'There is no doubt that the Adelaide Gallery . . . formed a species of school for the training of future restaurateurs who copied its methods down to such details as the plate glass mirrors and ruby-covered velveteen seats. It is almost impossible to go anywhere in London and the provinces without coming across restaurants fitted and equipped in the self-same style, and bearing outside the magic legend "So-and-so from Gatti's". Many of those worthy and enterprising gentlemen no doubt have never so much as set foot inside the Adelaide Gallery, but the use of the famous name only goes to show how magical is its attraction and what weight it still carries'. [*The Pelican*, 14 October 1906]

137 Edward Cecil, *Pagani's. The Artists' Room. 1871 - ?* (BBC News Information Service, 1957). *Kelly's Post Office Directory: London*, 1872, 1873. For a photograph of the interior of an elegant confectioners in 1902, see Sims, iii, p. 49.

138 Pascoe, *London of Today*, 1903 edition, p. 118.

139 Kinross, p. 24 quoting the *Illustrated London News* 27 December 1862.

140 Pascoe, *London of Today*, 1887 edition, p. 51. cf. Carlo Gatti 'built the well-known Hungerford Hall, which . . . was tastefully decorated, very much in the continental style . . . there was the attraction of a well-appointed band . . . the audience was admitted gratis; dominoes, drafts and chess were distributed on the tables, and the refreshments consisted mostly of coffee, chocolates, ice-creams, and sweet cakes.' The *Chimney Corner*, 17 December 1870.

141 Pascoe, *London of Today*, 1903 edition, p. 121. And cf. 'the London of today could hardly get on without its Swiss cafés . . . the Swiss café came, was seen and conquered; it came to stay and has become part and parcel of London life' (*'The Development of the Swiss Café'*, p. 434.)

142 Application of A & S Gatti for a wine and spirits licence, March 1878 [Greater London Record Office, Strand Division Middlesex Licensing Sessions MA/C/L/1878/94].

143 Pascoe, *London of Today*, 1887 edition, p.51.; 'Marcus Fall', *London Town: Sketches of London Life and Characters* (London: Tinsley Brothers, 1880),), i, p. 245; Cook, p. 291. Newnham-Davis, *Dinners and Diners*, p. 68.

144 Information from Joe Pedretti. Some marble tables were still to be found behind the scenes at Valchera's, the last of the Ticinese restaurants, in the 1980s (information from Peter Jacomelli).

145 Pascoe, *London of Today*, 1885 edition, p.51; 1903 edition, p.109. Newnham-Davies, pp. 67-8.

146 At least by men - Agostino and Stefano unsuccessfully tried to discourage women smokers: *Liverpool Post*, 14 October 1906.

147 'Marcus Fall', *London Town*, i, p. 249.

148 Olsen, p.103.

149 Obituaries of Stefano Gatti in the *Daily Telegraph*, *Daily Graphic* and *Daily Express* 13 October 1906 (which suggest that the youthful Agostino's pressure on Carlo was responsible for the introduction of 'chops and chips' in the late 1850s). Kinross, pp. 12 , 15 fig.5 (photograph of 129 Holborn Hill, c.1868).

150 Olsen, pp. 101, 103. Olsen's reliance on the architectural press led him to overlook the moderate-sized, architecturally insignificant Ticinese café-restaurants - including those of the Veglio, Marioni and Brentini families as well as the Gattis and the Bollas - that were in existence for several years before the building from 1865 onwards of monster restaurants such as the *Café Royal* and the revamped Gatti and Monico restaurants.

151 Greater London Record Office MA/C/L/1878/94.

152 Pascoe, *London of Today*, 1885 edition, p.45. An illustration of the Royal Adelaide Gallery [identified as 'Gattis' in the 1887 edition] on the facing page strengthens the identification.

153 'half-café and half-restaurant and wholly well conducted'. Pascoe, *London of Today*, 1892 edition, p. 61.

154 Information from Joe Bonetti and Raffaella Ferrari based on family knowledge. A photograph of the 1890s shows Ferrari's restaurant in Richmond advertising 'sandwiches' on the shop window [John Cloake, *Richmond Past* (Barnet: Historical Publications, 1991), p.90 ill. 161.] As late as 1935, the Ferrario Brothers' concern at Bexhill was described in the Post Office Directory as 'tea rooms'.

155 See Peter Jackson. *Walks in Old London* (London: Collins & Brown, 1993), pp.147 C (Giosue Giandoni, Kensington Church Street), 153 D (Agostino De Maria, Kensington High Street).

156 The large, commercial grill was supposedly one of Carlo Gatti's innovations (Kinross, p.12).

157 Pascoe, *London of Today*, 1885 edition, p. 47.

158 Pascoe, *London of Today*, 1889 edition, p.61. An anonymous, unidentified and undated newpaper cutting of the early 1880s describing The Royal Adelaide Gallery in the Philip Norman Collection, Guildhall Library, reveals that Gruyère was already the most popular cheese and that 150 plates of macaroni were served daily.

159 Ibid., p.56.

160 George and Weedon Grossmiths' great comic creation, Mr Pooter, the hero of *The Diary of a Nobody*, first published in 1892, lived in The Laurels, Brickfield Terrace, Holloway, which was precisely the district where several Ticinese

restaurants were to be found. For the Ticinese restaurants' middle-class clientele see Pascoe, 1892 edition, pp.66-7; Newnham-Davis (1899 edition), pp. 67-8. George Grossmith was a regular performer at the Adelphi Theatre (A & S Gatti's account at Coutts for the 1880s and 1890s records repeated payments to him) while George Grossmith Senior had been a regular visitor to Pagani's restaurant and signed one of the panels in the Artists' Room there.

161 Pascoe, *London of Today*, 1892 edition, p. 61.

162 'the best dishes here . . . (though the public apparently thinks differently) are now quite as dear as the leading West-end restaurants' Pascoe, *London of Today*, 1892 edition, p. 61 - and repeated in every later edition for the next decade, without making any dent in the Gattis' reputation for good value.

163 Menus owned by the Albertolli-Holland family.

164 Pascoe, 1885 edition, p. 52. Modern comparisons are difficult, but in 1900 £1 was a reasonable weekly salary.

165 *The Caterer and Hotel-Keeper Gazette*, 16 August 1897, p.438.

166 Newnham-Davis, 1899 edition, pp. 68, 72, 201, 250-252.

167 Pascoe, 1901 edition, p.137. The early menus of the Albertollis' *Swiss Café Restaurant* in Hastings confirm this. But while the cheapest dinner of 'one good plate per head of Roast Beef or Roast Mutton, Two Vegetables in Season, Tart, Cheese, Salad and a roll' cost 2s per head, the 'Up-to-Date Table d'Hote' menu consisting of oxtail or Julienne soup, fish (salmon), joints (beef or mutton), entrées (lamb cutlets 'à la jardinière'), poultry, three vegetables in season, dessert (stewed fruit and cream or jellies), cheese, salad and rolls cost 4s 6d.

168 *Survey of London*, 31 (1963), p. 74.

169 Newnham-Davis, 1899 edition, pp. 68-9, 72 (Adelaide Gallery), 298-300 (Pagani's), 248-250 (Monico's); *Survey of London* 31 (1963), p. 74 (Monico's); Peduzzi , pp. 81, 91-2 (photographs of the Royal Adelaide Gallery); *Caterer and Hotel-Keeper's Gazette*, pp. 434-439 [illustrations of Reggiori's]; Pascoe, 1887 edition, p. 44 (illustration of Royal Adelaide Gallery); Sims, i, pp.301 (text), 302 (illustration) (Royal Adelaide Gallery). An advertisement for the newly-opened Café Monico of 1878, in the very year that the Adelaide Gallery was completing its transformation into a restaurant, mentions all the standard features of the Ticinese café-restaurant: 'Grand Café Saloon. Grill Room. Best ventilated Billiard Saloons in London. Supper after the Theatres. Restaurant Open till Half-past 12' [quoted in *Survey of London*, 31 (1963), p. 74]. Newnham-Smith, pp. 248-50 conveys the impression that by 1898 the facilities were essentially unchanged though the restaurant had been enormously expanded in the interim.

170 Newnham-Davis, 1899 edition, p. 69; Cook, p. 290; Pascoe, 1887 edition, p. 51. The tokens had been distributed among the waiters before opening time. The waiters returned tokens equivalent to the price of the dishes ordered to the Gatti brothers as the dishes were being taken from the kitchens to the customer's table. At the end of the day the remaining tokens with the money (but excluding the tips which the waiters kept) were returned to the Gattis, thereby enabling the proprietors to check the honesty of their employees.

171 Newnham-Davis, 1899 edition, p.70; Pascoe, 1887 edition, p. 51; the anonymous article in the Philip Norman collection, Guildhall Library, gives a detailed description of the interior and functioning of the restaurant shortly after 1882. For illustrations see note 169.

172 *Survey of London*, 31 (1963), p. 74.

173 Pascoe, 1890 edition, p.72, 1892 edition, p.68.

174 The National Monuments Record contains a full set of photographs of the interiors and exteriors of c. 1900. Peduzzi p.91 (unidentified by Peduzzi but showing one of its suites being used for a Unione Ticinese dinner commemorating the centennial of Canton Ticino, 1903) and 161-3.

175 Pascoe, 1890 edition, p.72; 1901 edition, p.137.

176 *Shopping Notes and News*, November 1924, p. 98. It states that the restaurant opened in 1872. Cecil, however, more authoritatively gives the date as 1871.

177 Ibid., p. 99 (photograph) and p. 98 citing *The Architect's Journal*, 25 July 1923 and cf. Newnham-Davis, 1899 and 1901 editions, p. 299. Further illustrations in Peduzzi, pp. 158-9.

178 Newnham-Davis, 1899 edition, pp. 301-2. Sims, i; p. 303; ii, 346 (photograph), 348; Edward Cecil; *Shopping Notes and News*, p. 98 (photograph). The panels survived the destruction of the restaurant in October 1940 during the Blitz, because they were transferred to the keeping of the BBC. According to Meschini family tradition, one was supposedly taken by the royal family, because it contained the signatures of the later Edward VII and Lillie Langtry. The remainder were, briefly, displayed in the Castello Visconteo in Locarno in the 1950s and are now.in the home of the Meschini family in Ticino with the exception of three that were sold at Sotheby's (London) in the early 1990s.

179 *The Caterer and Hotel-Keeper's Gazette*, 16 August 1897, pp. 434-9 (numerous illustrations); The Camden Local Studies Archive and the National Monuments Record also have many photographs of the interior.

180 Pascoe, 1885 edition, p. 49.

181 Photographs owned by Peter Jacomelli. The *Café Royal* was first opened by Massimo Pazzi with money from the Gattis in 1874. It finally closed, when owned by Adolfo Pazzi, in 1953.

182 *Caterer and Hotel-Keeper's Gazette*, 16 August 1897, p. 437.

183 Copies of naturalisation papers from the Public Record Office in the possession of and kindly supplied by Bunny Veglio. The wording recalls Mrs. E.T. Cook's observation that the Ticinese waiters sought 'an honest competency . . . in middle age' through emigrating to England (Cook, p.289).

184 Memories of Signora Carla Bai, originally of Brissago, of her grandfather Vittorio Barosso who had worked as a waiter in London in his youth.

185 Samuel Butler, *Alps and Sanctuaries* (London: Jonathan Cape, 1881), p. 41.

186 Cook, pp. 288-9.

187 Information from Peter Jacomelli.

188 Bruni, p.71.

189 I am grateful to the Meschini family who allowed the authors to visit their villa, and offered them most generous hospitality, in the tradition of Pagani's, using its cutlery and on its crockery, and to Miss Shayler, a childhood friend from Hampstead Garden Suburb of Helen Sutcliffe née Meschini, who visited it in the early 1960s.

190 With a carved handshake symbolising honesty and the staff of Mercury symbolising trade. It was commissioned in 1883, presumably by his daughter Rosa, from Giovanni Chierici, professor at the Accademia di Belle Arte of Parma (I am grateful to Fernando Ferrari for this information).

191 *Chimney Corner*, 17 December 1870.

192 See Fernando Ferrari, 'Le meraviglie della sterlina: il ruolo politico dei Gatti in Ticino 1844-1893', in F. Ferrari (ed.), *Lo Zampino dei Gatti. Un capitolo di storia dell' emigrazione bleniese in Inghilterra* (Olivone: Fondazione Jacob-Piazza, 1996), pp. 131-133; Peduzzi, p. 58 incorrectly gives the dates 1839-1848.

193 In his later years he became increasingly radical in his views and, in 1875, he stood as a liberal. Local legend has it that his bitterness at being defeated led to his decision to be buried in Bellinzona rather than among the 'ungrateful' citizens of Dongio (see Ferrari, pp. 134-147).

194 Ferrari, pp.156-170; Peduzzi, p.77 wrongly gives 1872 as the start of his political career. And cf. Cook, p.290, who gives the year of his election as 1868.

195 Ferrari, pp.170-176; Peduzzi, p. 55. William Gatti, Agostino's great-grandson, possesses a book of newspaper cuttings assembled by Stefano in the late 1880s and 1890s, reflecting his interest in Ticinese politics (and particularly the liberal revolution of 1890) and his own political career (eg article from *The Referee*, 26 May 1889, p. 7 written by his close friend Henry Sampson). For the Ticinese political background see Raffaello Ceschi, *Ottocento Ticinese* (Locarno: Armando Dadò, 1986), pp. 48-61.

196 The ledgers of Coutts Bank show that while Carlo and Rosa Corazza gave money to the publishers of the liberal *Il Dovere*, Agostino and Stefano subscribed to the Conservative *Daily Telegraph*. A newspaper cutting in the possession of William Gatti shows that they were on close enough terms to visit the English Conservative leader, the Marquess of Salisbury, during a bout of illness in 1893. The ledgers also show that Agostino's widow and his daughter Maria regularly gave money to Catholic institutions and

197 Ferrari, pp.166-7, 172-3.

198 *Impavido* (Locarno, 28 January - 9 February 1871: three days before the cantonal elections). I am grateful to Fernando Ferrari for this information and see Bruni, p. 73.

199 Ferrari, pp. 183-4; obituaries of Stefano Gatti in the *Freier Rätier* and in the *Anzeiger von Uster*, 23 October 1906 and (more obliquely) in *The Sheffield Independent*, 15 October 1906. The *Freier Rätier* went so far as to claim that the liberals only secured a majority in the Val di Blenio once this practice ceased!

200 Giulio Rossi, Eligio Pometta, *Storia del Cantone Ticino* (revised edition ed. Giuseppe Martinola, Locarno: Armando Dadò, 1980), pp.343-8 (not mentioning Pazzi); protocols of Commune di Semione, 1891-6, Archivio Cantonale, Bellinzona. He is buried in Highgate Cemetery.

201 Ferrari, pp. 147-155.

202 Coutts Bank ledgers. The road, which was completed in 1877 though only formally opened in 1880, ran from Olivone at the head of the Val di Blenio into the neighbouring canton of Graubünden.

203 Kinross, pp. 44, 49.

204 Raffaello Ceschi, *Ottocento Ticinese* (Locarno: Armando Dadò, 1986), p. 162.

205 Mario Agliati, Giuseppe Mondada, Fernando Zappa, *Così era il Ticino* (Locarno: Armando Dadò, 1992), p. 33. The factory closed in the 1960s, but the buildings remain.

206 [Gambazzi], pp. 3, 4. In 1899 the Society voted another £50 to help the victims of another disaster at Airolo (ibid. p. 8). Cuttings in the possession of William Gatti from Ticinese newspapers show that Agostino and Stefano Gatti were making regular donations to similar good causes (eg the victims of natural disasters and nurseries) in their home village of Dongio.

207 *Kelly's Post Office Directories*: London, 1936, Margate 1936-7.

208 Carlo Gatti's Music Hall and Billiards Hall in Villiers Street had closed as early as 1903 and by 1906 the *Café de la Confédération Suisse* was described as 'a quiet little place now, with old-fashioned red plush seats and regular old customers' (obituary of Stefano Gatti in *The Manchester Guardian*, 13 October 1906). By 1939 *Gattis over the Water* had passed out of the family's hand and become a cinema, which was demolished following bomb damage in the later 1940s. The other Gatti enterprises continued. Even after nationalisation in 1948, the descendants of Agostino Gatti continued to be active in the electricity industry until the death of Stephen Geoffrey Gatti in 1958 (J.W. O'Connor, 'Early Pioneers', *Regional Power*, 4/1 (January 1961), pp. 6-11). Another grandson of Agostino, Jack [John Agostino Stefano] Gatti (1898-1972) sold the Adelphi Theatre in 1955 and the Vaudeville Theatre in 1969 (*Survey of London*, 36 (1970), p. 250; Vaudeville Theatre programme, 1994). 1981 saw the disappearance of United Carlo Gatti, the descendant of Carlo Gatti's ice-importing business (Angus McGill 'The Ice Man Goeth', *Evening Standard*, 11 November 1981; Peduzzi, pp. 118-128), but the heirs of the Corazza/Gatti only finally sold Carlo Gatti's house in Villiers Street in 1988 (Kinross, p. 42).

209 *Survey of London* 31 (1963), p. 74. All other information comes from Post Office directories.

210 Some of its stained glass is still to be seen in the McDonald's restaurant that now occupies the building.

211 At the very beginning of the 20th century, this was a problem for Charles Pascoe, who describes the various Ticinese-run restaurants that he mentions in his London guides as, interchangeably, Swiss, Italian and French.

212 Some unsuccessful Ticinesi seem to have ascribed their failure to English prejudice against foreigners and sought to revive their fortunes by anglicising their names. Giuseppe Gatti's grandson, Carlo Peduzzi, evidently hoped to improve the declining fortunes of his ancestral company, Gatti Bros chocolates, which had been founded in 1852, by renaming it 'C.P. Ducie' shortly before the First World War. Based at Ash Grove, Hackney, in East London it survived into the late 1920s (*Kelly Post Office Directories*; Peduzzi, pp. 68, 70-1 despite his incorrect statement (p. 63) that Gatti Bros and C.P. Ducie were distinct).

213 [Gambazzi], p. 6.

214 Tombstone in Olivone and oral tradition in the Ticinese colony of London.

215 Information from Raffaella Ferrari, his granddaughter.

216 Information from Frank Allegranza. His mother and Robert Belgeri (of Dongio) found it more profitable to let out rooms in Camden Town.

217 I am grateful to Mr Serse Cima, the son of the last proprietor, Giovanni Domenico, originally of Dangio, for this information. The business had been founded in 1885 and remained small enough to be classed as a confectioners after 1900, in contrast to Ferrari's restaurant in the same town.

218 Information from the late B.E. Albertolli.

219 Information from Raffaella Ferrari. Restaurants run by naturalised British subjects were, of course, unaffected.

220 Information from Joe Pedretti.

221 In 1881 Carlo Gatti's young widow Maria *née* Andreazzi married Frederico Scazziga who belonged to the family that ran the Park Hotel in Locarno (Coutts Bank ledgers). Adolfo Monico (1858-1931), a partner in Monico's restaurant, retired to Lugano where his son-in-law ran the Albergo Majestic (I am grateful to Joe Bonetti for this information), while the Meschini were involved with restaurants and hotels in Ticino and elsewhere before their period in England (I am grateful to Frances Meschini for this information).

222 London 18 December 1911 (Fiorini, 'Lettere', p.161 no.18).

223 'Oggi alle ore 9 del mattino ho celebrato mio matrimonio colla signorina Cecilia Legg, giovine Inglesa. . . Non è una giovine bella ne ricca, ma è in compenso . . . una buona lavoratrice ed economista più di me. . . Quanto a me, cara madre, non temete di nulla sebbene ammogliato con una giovine Inglese piuttosto che con una Svizzera o Francese non farà nessuna differenza, sarò sempre vostro figlio.' Luigi Togni to his mother, Putney, 4 June 1884 [Peter Jacomelli archive].

224 'soccorervi con consigli e denari e tutto quanto vi sarà necessario'. Information from Peter Jacomelli.

225 He is listed in the 1881 census as 'Giovanni Maria' and cf. Giovanni Pedrazzini to his parents 19 October 1877 (Pedrazzini, p.31) mentioning 'Giovanni' and his little brother 'Rocchino' [Rocco Giuseppe Stefano Gatti (1874-1950)].

226 *Who Was Who* 1929-1940, p. 500.

227 Not Cambridge as in Peduzzi, p. 105, who was also wrong to assert he was the first of his family to take British nationality. As Kinross discovered, Carlo had been naturalised in 1858.

228 Sir John was on the reformist wing of his party (*The Star*, 7 December 1926, 10 March 1927).

229 *Paris Times*, 5 March 1927. (William Gatti archive).

230 William Gatti possesses typescripts of her poems.

231 *Paris Times*, 5 March 1927 (William Gatti archive).

232 *The Times*, 16 September 1929.

233 *The Liverpool Post*, 12 March 1927 (William Gatti archive).

234 Will of Maria Gatti died 4 October 1951; will of Joan Lydia Maria Gatti, died 29 September 1971 (grants of probate, Somerset House and undated newspaper cutting owned by Fernando Ferrari).

235 The income from its sale was used to establish the *Fondo Fratelli Agostino & Stefano Gatti*, a charity which still survives (Ferrari, pp. 176-8).

236 Fiorini, p.155, no. 8.

Ticinese Restaurateurs & Chocolatiers in Central London 1847-1880

This list is derived from *Kelly's Post Office Directories* for central London for 1848-1880. Note that the Directories often record businesses only several years after their establishment and that several businesses are accidentally omitted, so that the figures represent an underestimate of the Ticinese businesses even in central London (though some Italian nationals may have been unwittingly included in the above list).   Except where stated, the list does not take into account the changes of street names and the renumbering of streets which occurred frequently between 1847-1875. This should, nevertheless, be borne in mind in the case of cafés etc. which appear to have moved (though several did move within the same road).

★   by a name indicates a founder-member of the Unione Ticinese in 1874.

For numbered notes see p. 36.

Adami, George
3 Sidney Place,
King's Road, SW
1858
129 King's Road, SW
1859-65

Agostino, Rolando
27 Shadwell High Street
1866-70

Alborghetti, John
205 City Road
1866-73

Alborghetti, Joseph
15 Pitfield Street, N
1878-

D'Alessandri, Atanasio[*1]
10 Black Prince Row,
Walworth Rd
1855-9
37 St. George's Place, SW
1861-
Craven Place, Kensington
1865-76

D'Alessandri, Eduardo
34 Aldersgate
1878-

D'Alessandri, Louis
2 Victoria Terrace,
Kennington Road, Lambeth
1865-8
110 Crawford Street,
Portman Square, W
1867-
220 Kennington Road,
Lambeth
1869-70
185A Marylebone Road
1871-

D'Alessandri, Nathaniel
169 Euston Road
1877-

Arcioni, Augusto
21 Goodge Street
1878-9
44 Goodge Street
1880

Dei Barthelmy
5 Upper Rupert Street, Soho
1871-5

Bellone
see Rodesano & Bellone

Bernasconi
see Tremaro & Bernasconi
see Debolla & Bernasconi

Bernasconi, Domenico
124 Old Kent Road
1865-8
131 Walworth Road
1869-

Bernasconi★ Bros
15 Titchborne Street
1867-8

Berti, Agostino★
56 Dudley Grove, Harrow
Road
1861-
93 Westbourne Grove,
Bayswater
1866-
307 Edgware Road
1872-
7 Margaret Terrace,
Harrow Road
1874
82A Bishop's Road, Bayswater
1874-
70 Norfolk Terrace, Bayswater
1876-
85 Westbourne Grove
1878-

Berti, Virgilio
133 Brompton Road, SW
1875-8

Bianchetti
see. Monico & Bianchetti

Bianchetti & Piazza
1 Station Buildings, Holloway
Road
1878-

Bianchi, Fernando
66 Church Lane, Whitechapel
1862-3
96 Fore Street, EC
1873-

Bianchi, Mrs Henrietta
62 Newington Butts
1880-

Bianchi, Martin
46 Chandos Street, WC
1880-

Bianchini, Joseph
18 Leader Street, Chelsea
1859-64

Bianchini, Mrs E
18 Leader Street, Chelsea
1865-6

Biffa, Battista
31 High Street, Notting Hill
Gate
1871-5
69 High Street, Notting Hill
Gate
1876-

Biucchi, Alexander
376 Oxford Street
1859-60

Biucchi
see Bolla & Biucchi

Bolla, Battista★
see Gatti, Carlo
1849-63
[without Gatti]
129 Holborn Hill
1864-
Holborn Buildings
1875

Bolla Pietro
91 Whitechapel High Street
1861
275 Strand
1880-

Bolla & Biucchi
156 St George Street, E
1878-

Bontrosi
See Fontana
1857

Borchi, Louis
62 Walcot Place, Kennington
1862-3

Braga, Domenico
16 Great Turnstile
1872-

Brentini, Ambrogio
37A St Martin's Lane
1872-

Brentini, Angelo
116 Crawford Street
1856-8

Brentini, Anthony & Giacomo
95 Whitechapel Road
1854-5
94 1/2 Whitechapel Road
1855-6
162 Shoreditch
1855-6

Brentini, Emanuele[*2]
112 Fleet Street
1880-

Brentini, Francesco★
116 (later 112) Fleet Street
1859-78
97 Holborn Hill
1859-60
100 Strand
1871-

Brentini, Giacomo
& see Brentini Anthony
1854-6
91 Fleet Street
1856-7
97 Holborn Hill
1861-70

Brentini, James
2 Boziers Court,
Tottenham Court Road
1861-70

Brentini, John
87 Kentish Town Road
1868-70
84 High Holborn
1871-3

Brentini, Luigi [3]
84 High Holborn
1874-

Brentini, Mrs Mary
22 St Martin's Court, WC
1880-

Brentini, Peter
22 Newgate Street, EC
1878-

Broggi & Maino
299 Holborn Hill
1856

Broggi, Luigi
292 High Holborn
1857

Brunetti, Carlo
14 Pont St, Belgrave Square
1859-67
4&5 Lower Grosvenor Place
1868-

Campioni
see Ciceri & Campioni
1875

Caraccio Bros.
87 Farringdon Street
1878-
141 Long Acre
1876-8

Caraccio, Constante
49 Borough High Street
1878-9
434 Strand
1878-

Caraccio & Pedretti
102A Essex Road, Islington
1869-70
116 Gray's Inn Road
1869-70
141 Long Acre
1869-70
87 Farringdon Road
1869-77
216 Pentonville Road
1869-

Carrocciero, Ambrogio*
198 Shoreditch High Street
1875-8
62 Bishopsgate Without
1876-7
32 Bishopsgate Without
1878-80

Carrocciero, John
718 Old Kent Road
1867-70
502 Mile End Road
1871-9
486 Mile End Road
1880

Carrocciero, Charles & John
32 Bishopsgate Without
1880-

Carati, Natale
10 Black Prince Row,
Walworth
1866
45 Walworth Road
1867-73

Cattaneo, Peter
37 Norton Folgate, NE
1869-71
113 Upper Whitecross, EC
1872

Ciceri, Luigi
33 City Road
1879-

Ciceri & Campioni
65 Walworth Road
1875-
20 New Kent Road
1876-
32 New Kent Road
1880

Cimelli, Joseph
249 Portobello Road
1875-

Cizzio Bros
26 High Street,
Notting Hill Gate
1877-

Cizzio, Domenico & Sons
24 Edgware Road
1867-8
56 Edgware Road
1869-70

Conceprio, Luke
61 Hampstead Road
1864
22 High Street, St John's
Wood
1873-

Corazza, Giacomo
218 Westminster Bridge Road
1879-

Cortesi, Antonio
84 Hackney Road
1862-3
87 Upper Street, Islington
1863
307 Hackney Road
1864

Cortesi, Joseph*
91 Whitechapel High Street
1862
97 Whitechapel Road
1863-
179 Whitechapel Road
1866-7
19 & 20 Aldgate High Street
1876-

Cortesi & Fusi
97 Whitechapel Road
1875

Cortesi & Jacomelli
8 Middle Row, High Holborn
1862
246 High Holborn
1862
9 Newgate Street, EC
1862

D'Alessandri
see Alessandri

Debolla, B.
118 Whitechapel High Street
1860-1

Debolla, Bartholomew
107 Edgware Road
1864-8
252 Edgware Road
1869

Debolla, Battista
116 Upper Street, Islington
1867
144 Holborn Bars
1870-
252 Edgware Road
1870-
28 Hammersmith Broadway
1871-6
15 Great Turnstile Street.
Holborn
1874-5
32 King Street
1874-5
111 High Holborn
1876-9
233 Tottenham Court Road
1877-
166B Oxford Street
1878-

Debolla, Carlo
376 Oxford Street
1868-

Debolla, Joseph
122 Whitechapel High Street
1861

Debolla & Bernasconi
111 High Holborn
1880

Debolla & Derighetti, Carlo
376 Oxford Street
1861-2

Debolla & Martinali
376 Oxford Street
1863-7

Debolla & Yiamini (sic)
107 Edgware Road
1863

Dei Barthelmy
see Barthelmy

Dell'Oro & Torriani
135 Tottenham Court Road
1864-70

Dell'Oro, Stefano*4
135 Tottenham Court Road
1871, 1874-

Dell'Oro, Stefano & Eurietti
135 Tottenham Court Road
1872-3

De Maria
see Maria

De Negri
see Negri

Derighetti, Carlo
& see Debolla & Derighetti
Simona & Derighetti

Diviani, Clemente
426 & 428 Euston Road
1871-

Diviani, Daniel
100 Pentonville Road
1875-

Diviani, Emanuele
19 Upper King Street, WC
1864
47 Holloway Road
1865
2 York Place, Kingsland Road
1866
497 Kingsland Road
1867-70
9 Finsbury Park Terrace,
Seven Sisters Rd
1871

Diviani, George
79 Church Street, Chelsea
1869-70

Diviani, Giovanni
42 Wilderness Row,
Clerkenwell (?)
1856-60
428 Euston Road
1861-70
108 Crawford Street
1862
5 Sidney Place,
Commercial Road
1862-3
47 Holloway Road
1866
169 Euston Road
1874-

Diviani, Giuseppe
137 City Road
1864-
47 Holloway Road
1867-79
404 Holloway Road
1873-

Diviani, Guglielmo
98 Pentonville Road
1867
100 Pentonville Road
1868-74

Diviani, Paul
497 Kingsland Road
1871

Diviani & Togni
474 Kingsland Road
1871

Donetta, John
102 Park Street,
Camden Town
1873-
& see Veglio & Donetta

Eurietti
see Dell'Oro & Eurietti
1872-
see (De) Maria & Eurietti
(Jurietti) (?)
1871-

Eurietti, Natale
4 Shepherdess Walk
1873-
& see Jurietti (?)

Fasola, John
249 Caledonian Road
1864-73

Ferrari, Carlo*5
91 Whitechapel High Street
1864-5

Ferrare (sic), Giacomo
108 Goswell Road, EC
1861-2
141 Goswell Road
1863

Ferrari, Giuseppe
51 Chalk Farm Road
1864-5

Ferrari
see Fusi
1863

Ferrario & Feloj
183 Fleet Street
1856

Ferrario, Joseph
77 Holborn Hill
1862-3
181 Fleet Street
1865-6

Ferrario, Natale
103 Holborn Hill
1854-67
102 Borough High Street
1857-70
8 Middle Row, Holborn
1859

Ferrario, Natale (contd)
120 Newgate Street
1861-74
183 Fleet Street
1862-3
19 Stafford Row, Pimlico
1863-8
181 Fleet Street
1867-75
5 Buckingham Palace Road
1869-70
1 Buckingham Palace Road
1871-

Ferrario, Raphael
49A Great Queen Street, WC
1860

Fontana & Bontrosi
210 Strand
1857

Fontana, Ferdinando*6
2 Brompton Terrace, SW
1859
1 Brompton Terrace, SW
1860
51 Golbourne Road
1876-

Fontana, Pietro
7 Little Compton Street, Soho
1876-8
71 Hyde Road, Hoxton
1878-9

Fontanelli, Joseph
181 Portobello Road
1871-2

Formaggia & Menegalli
87 Tottenham Court Road
1881

Fusi & Ferrari
2 Caroline Place,
Hampstead Road
1863

Fusi
see Cortesi & Fusi
1875

Fuso, Louis
246 High Holborn
1875-

Gallizia
see Piazza & Gallizia

Galo, Joseph
9 Wellington Terrace,
Elgin Road, SW
1868-70

Gatti Bros (chocolates)
149 Minories
1875

Gatti, Agostino & Carlo
see Gatti, Carlo

Gatti, Agostino & Monico
(Giacomo)
Royal Adelaide Gallery
1863-70

Gatti, A. & Stefano & Monico
(G & B)
Royal Adelaide Gallery
1871-2

Gatti, Agostino* & Stefano*7
Royal Adelaide Gallery
1873-1939

Gatti, Carlo*
30 Great Hall, Hungerford
Market
1848-53
29,61 Great Hall, Hungerford
Market
1849-53
32-34 Great Hall, Hungerford
Market
1854-62
3 Great Hall, Hungerford
Market
1855-7
90 (later 91)
Whitechapel High Street
1855-60
7 Edgware Road
1856-8
31 Great Hall, Hungerford
Market
1856-62
254 Oxford Street
1856-8
62 Great Hall, Hungerford
Market
1857-8
61 Great Hall, Hungerford
Market
1857-62
152 Oxford Street
1857
76 Bridge Road, Lambeth
1864-6
214 Westminster Bridge Road,
Lambeth
1865-
52 Strand
1865-
Railway Arches, Villiers Street
1868-
& Gatti, Agostino
3, 32-4 Great Hall,
Hungerford Market
1855
& Bolla, Battista
129 Holborn Hill
1849-63
122 Holborn Hill
1850-60

Gatti (Carlo and Giuseppe)
and Monico (Giuseppe)
as above properties for
1859-63

Gatti, Domenico
12 Frederick's Place, Old Kent
Road, SE 1862-3
124 Old Kent Road, SE
1864
69 Chalk Farm Road
1864-76
140 Essex Road, Islington
1866-7
10 Haverstock Hill
1877-

Gatti, Joseph
13 Aldgate
1853-73
18 Aldgate
1856-60
67 Blackman Street, Borough
1855-6
9 Silver Street, Greenwich
1858

Gatti, Luca8
6 Upper Queen's Building,
SW
1863
153 Brompton Road
1864-

Gatti & Rodesino
166 Strand
1878-

Gianella, Francesco*
71 Norfolk Terrace, Bayswater
1880-

Gianella
see Sorgesa & Gianella

Gianella Bros
68 Strand
1874-

Gianelli, Giovanni
254 Oxford Street
1863-6
123 Walworth Road
1873
307 Fulham Road, SW
1874-

Gianora
see Scheggia & Gianora

De Giorgi, Pietro
23 Titchborne St, Haymarket
1857

De Giorgi, Torriani & Co.
23 Titchborne St, Haymarket
1858

Giuliani, Antoine
153 St John's Street,
Clerkenwell
1875-

Guidinetti, P.
23 Titchborne St, Haymarket
1859

Guidinetti & Beretta
23 Titchborne St, Haymarket
1860

Jacomelli, Ambrose
246 High Holborn
1871-5
178 Westminster Bridge Road
1877-

Jacomelli, Battista
2 Walworth Place,
Walworth Road
1863-4
67 1/2 Blackman Street,
Borough
1865-7
233 Tottenham Court Road
1869-70

Jacomelli, Carlo
246 High Holborn
1863-6
8 Middle Row, High Holborn
1867

Jacomelli, Joseph
10 Black Prince Row,
Walworth
1860-5

Jacomelli, Louis
8 Middle Row, High Holborn
1863-70

Jacomelli
see also Cortesi & Jacomelli

Jemini, James *9
72 Drury Lane
1868-
54 Haymarket
1874-

Juliani, Antoine
see Giuliani

Jurietti & De Maria
see (De) Maria & Eurietti

Jurietti, Nathaniel
29 Beech Street, Barbican
1872-3
363 King's Road, Chelsea
1878-

Kiber (Daniele?)* & Metalli,
(Antonio?)*
27A Villiers Street
1876-

Lazzari, John
26 Church Lane, Whitechapel
1864-74
156 St George Street, E
1880-

Lussi, Basilico*
see Mentasti & Lussi

Maino
see Broggi
1856

Malloni, Sebastiano
& Polti Bros
71 Camberwell Road, SE
1878-
475 Cambridge Road, E
1878-

De Maria, Agostino
4 Shepherdess Walk
1868-71
47 High Street, Camden
Town
1872-8
216 Pentonville Road
1874
51 Islington High Street
1874-7
13 High Road, Knightsbridge
1876-
329 Hoxton Street
1878-9
74 Islington High Street
1878-

De Maria, Giacomo
20 Paul Street, Finsbury
1877-
82 Chiswell Street, EC
1880-
41 Walworth Street, SE
1880-

De Maria, Giuseppe
187A Sloane Street
1860

De Maria & Eurietti/Jurietti
82 Chiswell Street EC
1871-9
29 Beech Street, EC
1871

Marioni, Domenico*
3A Union Place North
1857
74 Marylebone Road
1858
76 Marylebone Road
1859-63
7 Edgware Road
1859, 1861
254 Oxford Street
1859
1861-2
1866-72
15 Titchborne Place,
Haymarket
1859-66

Marioni, Giovanni Domenico*
24 Edgware Road
1861-70
27A Villiers Street
1873-5
25 Villiers Street
1874-

Marioni, Giuseppe
see Marioni, Joseph

Marioni, John
316 Strand
1877-

Marioni, Joseph
4 Pleasant Row, Pentonville
1855-7
4 Bridge Street, Lambeth
1855-64
260A Strand
1856-64
23 Great Russell Street
1856
34 Fish Street. Hill, EC
1856-75
232 Pentonville Rd
1858-73
231 Shoreditch High Street
1858-64
56 Bridge Rd, Lambeth
1858-64
79A Goswell Road, EC
1858
221 Piccadilly
1859-70
198 Shoreditch High Street
1860-73
4 Aldgate
1860-73
170 Bishopsgate Without
1860-71
13 High Road, Knightsbridge
1861-3

Marioni, Joseph (contd)
135 Tottenham Court Road
1861-2
132 Upper Thames Street
1861-5
21 Fish Street Hill
1863-5
178 Westminster Bridge Road,
Lambeth
1865-76
274 Westminster Bridge Road,
Lambeth
1865-
30 Coventry Street, W
1865-70
109 Upper Thames Street
1866-
133 Brompton Road
1866-73
13 High Road, Knightsbridge
1867-73
Queen's Pavilion, Primrose
Hill
1869-
32 Bishopsgate Without
1872-

Marioni, Louis*
232 Pentonville Road
1869-73

Marioni, Thomas George
322 Holloway Road
1874-

Marioni & Orlandini
8 High Street,
Notting Hill Gate
1866-

Marioni & Rodesano
14 Oxford Street
1874-

Martinali
see Debolla & Martinali

Menegalli, Joseph[10]
18 Shaftesbury Terrace,
Vauxhall Bridge Street
1863

Menegalli, Carlo
see Formaggia & Menegalli

Mentasti Bros
31 King William Street, EC
1871-2
3 Coventry Street, W
1878-

Mentasti & Lussi
113 Westbourne Grove
1877-
see also Monico & Mentasti

Metalli
see Kiber & Metalli

Monico Bros.
254 Oxford Street
1860
7 Edgware Road
1860
1 Brompton Terrace,
Brompton Rd
1861-3
133 Brompton Road, SW
1865

Monico Bros.(contd)
27 Bell Street, Edgware Road
1866-70
1A New Church Street,
Westminster, NW
1866-70
95 Church Street, Lisson
Grove
1871-2

Monico, Battista
and see Gatti & Monico

Monico, Giacomo*
and see Gatti & Monico

Monico, Giacomo* & Battista
15 Titchborne Street
1877-

Monico, Giuseppe
Knightsbridge [acc. Kinross]
1858
[refers to actual opening date
of 1 Brompton Terrace?]
and see Gatti, Carlo

Monico, John A.
1A New Church Street, NW
1865

Monico, Luigi
110 Crawford Street,
Marylebone
1880

Monico & Mentasti
28 Aldgate
1872

Monico & Bianchetti
23 Aldgate
1873-

Morganti, Lawrence
163 Cambridge Road, NE
1868-74
266 High Holborn
1875-
134 Edgware Road
1880

Morganti, Peter
87 Tottenham Court Road
1879-80

Moriccia & Bordessa
19 Exmouth Street, SW
1863

Moriccia, Anthony
19 Exmouth Street, SW
1864-5

Moriggia, Anthony
463 Hackney Road, NE
1864-5
10 London Road, Southwark
1865-10
1/2 Islington High Street
1866-77
116 Upper Street, Islington
1871-3
21 Islington High Street
1878-

Moriggia, Charles
231 Westminster Bridge Road
1871-78

Moriggia, John
173 Newington Butts
1867-78
231 Westminster Bridge Road
1868-70

Moriggia, Peter
191 High Holborn
1858
82 1/2 High Street,
Camden Town
1860-4
10 1/2 High Street, Islington
1862-5
240 Euston Road
1863
172 High Street,
Camden Town
1865-
46 Chandos Street, WC
1869-70

Mutal, Joseph
26 Langley Place,
Commercial Rd
1857
see also Rodesino
1855-6

Nadale, Peter
176 Lambeth Walk
1866

Nadale, Simon
160 Caledonian Road
1876-

Negri, Augustin De
16 Great Turnstile, WC
1868-70
124 Old Kent Road
1869-70
44 Theobalds Road
1872
216 Pentonville Road
1873-

Natti, Peter
86-7 Farringdon Street
1864-6

Offredi, Angelo
474 Kingsland Road, NE
1867-70

Oreggia, Vincent[11]
Boziers Court,
Tottenham Court Road
1873-75
335 Strand
1875-

Orlandini
see Marioni & Orlandini
1866

Pagani Bros
10 Silver Street,
Golden Square
1875-6

Pagani, Charles
31 High Holborn
1876-

Pagani, Isidoro*[12]
13 High Street, Knightsbridge
1874-76

Pagani, Luigi[*12]
400 Euston Road
1879-

Pagani, Mario[*13]
54 Great Portland Street
1873-

Panzeri, John
67 1/2 Blackman Street,
Borough
1868-70
53 Whitechapel High Street
1871
66 West Smithfield
1873-78
2 Blackman Street, Borough
1874-78
83 Newington Causeway
1874-76

Panzeri Bros
49 Borough High Street
1879-
2 Blackman Street, Borough
1879-
66 West Smithfield
1879-
1 Great Dover Street
1879
343 Goswell Street
1879-

Panzini, George
116 Pentonville Road
1868-70

Panzini, John
116 Pentonville Road
1867

Pedretta, Manfredo
87 Upper Street, Islington
1874

Pedretti, Caraccio & Co
see Caraccio & Pedretti
1869-71

Piazza, Vincenzo[*14]
41 St George's Place,
Knightsbridge
1879-

Piazza & Gallizia
41 St George's Place,
Knightsbridge
1876-78

Pelli, John
46 Queen Street, Pimlico
1871-3

Polli, Angela
43 Great Windmill Street,
Soho
1878-79

Polli, Carlo
11 Minories
1879-
43 Great Windmill Street,
Soho
1880-

Polli, Giuseppe
52 Old Compton Street, Soho
1869-73

Polli, Marco
301 Goswell Road
1880-

Polli, Mario
4 Aldgate
1879-
7 Aldgate
1879-

Polli, Matthew
4 Aldgate
1873- 75

Polli Bros
11 Minories
1875-78
4 Aldgate
1876-78
7 Aldgate
1878

Polti
see Malloni & Polti

Polti Bros
71 Camberwell Road, SE
1879-

Pozzi, Pietro
46 Chandos Street, WC
1871-2
11A (later 9) Princes Street,
Leicester Square
1871-4

Protti, Stefano[*]
2 Old Compton Street, Soho
1865

Puzzi Bros
216 Pentonville Road
1877-
222 High Street,
Camden Town
1877-

Reggiori, Luigi[*] & Pietro[*15]
272-4 Grays Inn Road
1881
269, 271 Pentonville Road
1881

Roddiselliso, H.
29 Lennon Street,
Goodman's Fields
1860

Rodesano
see Marioni & Rodesino

Rodesano, John
163 Bishopsgate Without
1859-
211 Shoreditch High Street
1860
18 Upper Street, Islington
1861
15 Titchborne Street,
Haymarket
1865-70
73 Regent's Park Road
1869-70

Rodesano & Belloni
127 Kentish Town Road
1879-

Rodesino, Joseph[*]
14 Oxford Street
1871-3

Rodesino, Luigi & Mutal,
Joseph
14 Bishopsgate Without
1855-6

Rodesino, Luigi
141 Bishopsgate Without
1857-8

Rodesino, Luke[*16]
120 Shoreditch High Street
1871-3
73 Regents Park Road
1872-

Rossi, Nicola
2 Old Compton Street, Soho
1869

Rossi, Serafino
6 Queen's Road, Chelsea
1863

Salvi, Peter
105 Hackney Road
1873-

Sarto, Samuel
308 Euston Road
1859-60

Scheggia, Giulio[*]
133 Brompton Road
1880-

Scheggia & Gianora
133 Brompton Road
1879

Simona, Joseph[*]
272 Grays Inn Road
1875-80
269 Pentonville Road
1875-80
313 Grays Inn Road
1877-

Simona, Pietro
44 Gt Windmill Street,
Haymarket
1857-8

Simona & Derighetti
1 Station Buildings,
Holloway Road
1877

Sorgesa, Carlo[*17]
9 Queen's Road, Bayswater
1875-7
25 Queen's Road, Bayswater
1878-9

Sorgesa, John
102 Park Street,
Camden Town
1863
144 Camden High Street
1864-70

Sorgesa, Giuseppe[*]
497 Kingsland Road
1878-

Sorgesa & Gianella
497 Kingsland Road
1875-77

Togni
see Diviani & Togni
1871

Torriani, Carlo
385 Euston Road
1880-

Torriani
see (De) Giorgi
see Dell'Oro

Torriano, Peter
54 Great Portland Street
1871

Tremaro & Bernasconi
16 Mount Pleasant Road,
Liverpool Street
1864

Valentini Bros.
76 Marylebone Road
1864-72

Valentini, Fernando
76 Marylebone Road
1873
34 Fish Street Hill
1876-

Valentini, John
10A The Terrace,
Kensington Road
1876-

Valentini, John & Fernando
51 Chalk Farm Road
1867-70
10 The Terrace
Kensington Road
1872-75

Vanina, Rodolfo[*18]
69 Chalk Farm Road, NW
1877-

Veglio Bros
405 Oxford Street
1862-

Veglio, Charles[*]
431 Oxford Street
1858
17 Tottenham Court Road
1858-
330 Euston Road
1871-
102 Park Street
Camden Town
1871

Veglio, John
330 Euston Road
1864-70
102 Park Street
Camden Town
1864-70
314 & 316 Euston Road
1871-

Veglio, Nazaro
405 Oxford Street
1859-61

Veglio, Vincenzo
21 Goodge Street
1877-
6 Bishop's Road, W
1880

Veglio & Donetta
6 Bishop's Road, W
1877-79

Venazzi, Peter
233 Tottenham Court Road
1867-69

Yolli, Francis
24 Edgware Road
1865

Zeglio, Charles*
51 Chalk Farm Road
1866

Zeglio, Charles & Luigi*
3 Coventry Street, W
1875-76

Notes to listing of restaurateurs

1 1828-1909 (information from Joe Bonnetti).
2 1850-1893 (ditto)
3 1845-1911 m. Giuseppina Taddei. 84 High Holborn was a sandwich bar. Later had restaurants in Edgware Road (later owned by Divianis) and at 80 Westbourne Grove (to 1904). Buried in Kensal Green (information from Joe Bonnetti).
4 First Treasurer of the Unione Ticinese.
5 Ice worker of same name listed at Gatti's, New Wharf Road, census of 1871.
6 1830-1884. Buried in Kensal Green.

7 Founder president of the Unione Ticinese.
8 b. 1843, listed as waiter at Hungerford Market, census of 1861.
9 d. 1908.
10 b. 1837. Listed as waiter, Hungerford Market, census of 1861.
11 b. 1849/50. Listed as waiter, Royal Adelaide Gallery, census of 1871.
12 b. 1828. Listed as cook, Royal Adelaide Gallery, census of 1871.
13 First Vice-President of Unione Ticinese.
14 b. 1847/8. Listed as billiard marker, Royal Adelaide Gallery, census of 1871. First Secretary of the Unione Ticinese.

15 1854-1908. Buried in Kensal Green near Gatti tomb.
16 1832-1888. Buried in Unione Ticinese grave, Kensal Green.
17 1846-1879. Buried in Unione Ticinese grave, Kensal Green.
18 1847-1889. Original Unione Ticinese committee member. Listed as waiter at Gatti's-over-the-Water music hall, census of 1871. Buried in Unione Ticinese grave, Kensal Green.

Bibliography

1. **Primary sources**

Albertolli-Holland family archives.
Joe Bonetti family archives.
Serse Cima family archives.
Coutt's Bank: Ledgers for the accounts of members of the Gatti family.
De Maria family archives.
Will Gatti archives.
Peter Jacomelli archives.
Public Record Office (census returns, 1851-1891).
Veglio family papers.

2. **Printed sources and secondary literature**

Mario Agliato, Giuseppe Mondada, Fernando Zappa, *Cosi era il Ticino* (Locarno: Armando Dadò, 1992).
Anon.,The Development of the Swiss Café in London.
A Visit to Reggiori's Restaurants', *The Caterer and Hotel-Keeper's Gazette*, 16 August 1897.
Baedeker's Switzerland, 9th ed. (Leipzig: Carl Baedeker, 1881).
Gianni Berla, 'Migranti ticinesi a Parigi (1830-1850), *Archivio Storico Ticinese*, xxviii (1991), pp. 97-146.
Piero Bianconi, *Lettere di Giovanni Pedrazzini ai Familiari* (Locarno: Pedrazzini, 1973).
Samuel Butler, *Alps and Sanctuaries* (London: Jonathan Cape, 1881).
Carlo Bonetti, *Along a High Way of History. National Museum of the St. Gotthard* (Bellinzona: St. Gotthard Foundation, 1989).
Federico Bruni, *I Cioccolatieri. Dall'Artigianato all'Industria* (Bellinzona: S. A. Grassi & Co., 1946).
Edward Cecil, *Pagani's. The Artists' Room 1871-?* (London: BBC news Information Service, 1957).
Raffaello Ceschi, *Ottocento Ticinese* (Locarno: Armando Dadò,1986).
Raffaello Ceschi, 'Bleniesi Milanesi. Note sull'emigrazione di mestieri dalla Svizzera Italiana', *Col bastone e la bisaccia per le strade d'Europa. Migrazioni stagionali di mestiere dell'arco alpino nei secoli xvi-xviii* . Atti di un seminario di studi tenutosi a Bellinzona l'8 e il 9 settembre 1988. (Bellinzona: Edizioni Salvioni, 1991), pp. 49-72.
Terri Colpi, *The Italian Factor. The Italian Community in Great Britain* (Edinburgh: Mainstream, 1991)
Charles Dickens, jr. *Dickens's Dictionary of London*, 13th edition (London: Charles Dickens & Evans, 1891-2).

E.T. Cook, *Highways and Byways in London* (London: Macmillan, 1902).
Ferdinando Cesare Farra & Giuseppe Gallizia, 'L'Emigrazione dalla Val Blenio a Milano attraverso i secoli', *Archivio Storico Lombardo*, 1961, pp. 117-130.
Fernando Ferrari (ed.), *Lo Zampino dei Gatti. Un capitolo di storia dell'emigrazione bleniese in Inghilterra* (Olivone: Fondazione Jacobo Piazza, 1996).
Sonia Fiorini, 'Lettere di emigranti bleniesi in Inghilterra', *Archivio Storico Ticinese*, xxviii (1991), pp. 147-164.
Andreas Furger, *Der Gotthard Postwagen* (Zurich: Schweizersiches Landesmuseum, 1990).
[Oscar Gambazzi], *Sessant'anni di Vita Ticinese a Londra. Breve rassegna storica in occasione del 60mo anniversario della sua Fondazione 1874-1934* (London: Unione Ticinese, 1934).
David R. Green, 'Little Italy in Victorian London. Holborn's Italian Community'. *Camden History Review* 15 (1988), pp. 2-6.
Kelly's Post Office Directories 1847-1987.
Leigh's New Picture of London or, a view of the political, religious, medical, literary, municipal commercial and moral state of the British Metropolis (London: Samuel Leigh, 1827).
Murray's Handbook for Travellers in Switzerland (London: John Murray & Son, 1838).
Lieut.-Col. Newnham-Davis, *Dinners and Diners. Where and How to Dine in London* (London: Grant Richards, 1899; 2nd ed., 1901).
Donald J. Olsen, *The Growth of Victorian London* (London: Batsford, 1976), pp. 93-111.
Charles Eyre Pascoe, *London of Today* (London: Sampson Low, Searle & Rivington, 1885-1907).
Pino Peduzzi, *Pioneri Ticinesi in Inghilterra. La Saga della Famiglia Gatti 1780-1980* (Bellinzona: Casagrande, 1985)
George R. Sims, *Living London* (London: Cassell, 1903).
Lucio Sponza, 'The Italians in London', in Nick Merriman (ed.) *The Peopling of London. Fifteen Thousand Years of Settlement from Overseas* (London: Museum of London, 1993), pp. 129-137.
Survey of London, 31 [St James's Westminster] (London: Survey of London Committee, 1963).
Survey of London, 36 [St Paul's, Covent Garden] (London: Survey of London Committee, 1970).